Goodbye, Mr. Taxman

Goodbye, Mr. Taxman

MOOSE SALOMAN

Copyright © 2018 by Moose Saloman.

Library of Congress Control Number:		2018903694
ISBN:	Hardcover	978-1-9845-1632-9
	Softcover	978-1-9845-1631-2
	eBook	978-1-9845-1630-5

All rights reserved. No part of this book may be reproduced or transmitted in any form or by any means, electronic or mechanical, including photocopying, recording, or by any information storage and retrieval system, without permission in writing from the copyright owner.

Any people depicted in stock imagery provided by Getty Images are models, and such images are being used for illustrative purposes only. Certain stock imagery © Getty Images.

Print information available on the last page.

Jacket Design by the Author

Rev. date: 04/28/2018

To order additional copies of this book, contact:
Xlibris
1-888-795-4274
www.Xlibris.com
Orders@Xlibris.com

Contents

Introduction ix

The Inspiration 1
What Is Wrong With Our Present Economic System? ... 3
Objectives 9
How Did We Get Where We Are? 17
The Basics: Our Economic System Should Be Consistent With The Laws Of Nature 19
We Are Not Genetically Created Equal 25
What Is Wealth? 31
Inflation 34
James Smart And Timothy Slim 36
Overhauling The System 39
Taxes 47
Healthcare 53
Education 60
Student Loans 64
Disaster Recovery Funds 65
Rebuilding Infrastructure 66
Support For The Unemployed And Low Earners 68

Research And Development	69
Retirement Social Security	73
Insurance	75
Utilities	79
Food	81
Transportation	83
Defense	84
International Debt	86
Charity	87
The Steering Seven	88
Implementation	90
The Private Sector	93
Wall Street	95
The Fed	97
Immigration	100
Foreign Aid	103
Export And Import	104
The Supreme Court	106
Choosing Our Leaders	108
Overcoming Side Effects	111
Conclusion	115
Index	123

Dedicating this book to the poor and the economically deprived among us.

Introduction

The never-ending economic upheavals in our world—causing depressions, recessions, and bubbles and creating untold hardships and misery to the human race—cries out for that urgent need to reexamine the validity of our existing, clearly harmful economic system and make appropriate changes.

And so the intent of writing this book is to sound off a wake-up call to my fellow humans, to stress that our existing economic system, to meet our today's and future living needs, is totally flawed and should be discarded as a worn-out, shredded garment.

With the prevailing economic undercurrents and the embedded dynamics in the system—among them the growing effects of technology, such as the Internet, the automation, which can vastly increase productivity, the upcoming onslaught of artificial intelligence through robotics, and other brewing inventions, all of these have created an unstoppable wave of killing jobs and, in the long run, will kill more jobs than they can create.

With the shrinking of job availability, which, in turn, would increase unemployment and lower the collection of the feeble income-tax relative to our growing needs, it will become more and more difficult to collect sufficient money to attend to society's vital needs. Moreover, it will further curtail our progress in other urgent programs, such as NASA's (National Aeronautics and Space Administration) ability to track and destroy or divert those dangerous space intruders—asteroids and meteors to prevent them from hitting the earth and causing unmanageable destruction. Thus, from all aspects, to continue embracing our current totally unjustifiable economic system and eventually fall off the cliff should earn us wearing the crown of stupidity.

History clearly shows that in the beginning, money was invented to be used as a measuring unit of value—just like pounds, yards, etc.—to represent the quantity of value of what we have earned and now own as individuals for bartering purposes among ourselves, to acquire goods and services. Obviously, to this end, for the present time, we all have to work to earn the money we need.

Nevertheless, there are still other living needs that should be provided by our government, which would require money, among them building roads and bridges, maintaining armies and protective defense equipment, and setting up educational facilities nationwide and other services needed by us as a society. Also, we need to lend a hand to the unemployed, the needy, and the handicapped.

We should provide ready and open access to healthcare as well as emergency assistance to those impacted by sudden natural disasters, such as floods, earthquakes, and other unexpected catastrophes. Under our existing economic system, the earners among us are required to chip in parts of their earnings in the form of income-tax to meet society's needs.

In this book, I will lay out the appropriate, realistic, and ironclad solution to change our dreaded existing economic system and adopt the plan that we should have been following all along, which will open the gates of prosperity throughout our country and also encourage other nations to follow our footsteps. The proposed change will be practical, reasonable, and consistent with the rules of Mother Nature. It will enable us to discard the present economic system. Most importantly, it will give all of us free access to healthcare and higher education and help us pursue other vital projects to propel us into the future. We will be able to upgrade the infrastructure, intensify research and development to unlock the secrets of Mother Nature, and do all that we want to improve our quality of life without worrying about the overpowering curse of money.

Nevertheless, from the start, I can predict without a doubt that my plan will be met by economists and politicians with much skepticism, ridicule, and even laughter. Most likely, they will oppose the new economic system on the grounds that it will weaken the value of our currency. Needless to say the least, I'm neither a trained scientist nor an economist and have no track record in this field. It's simply the product of my life's observations and experiences in dealing with economic ups and downs and the hardships imposed on us that prompted me to question the validity of our prevailing system and learn how and why it was thrusted upon humanity.

Furthermore, we should examine to see whether our present economic system is indeed necessary and appropriate, whether we could and should get out of it, and what would be the most appropriate system to follow. But needless to say, that what I am proposing is not something outlandish. It is already there. Then why we have been shying away from it?

Other objections to my plan might stem from the lack of readiness to embrace such a simple and realistic system, consistent with the laws of nature, and because of the transitional difficulties that some objectors may bring up.

However, I feel confident that in time, this plan will eventually be adopted because under its basic tenets, no human in our country will be left behind, economically deprived. Indeed, it will open the floodgates of prosperity and change the way of life for humankind. No need for any of us to go hungry, without shelter, without access to healthcare, and without higher education due to lack of money. It will usher an era of economic harmony and comfort of life to all of us, rich and poor, and pave the way to a safer mode of living on our precious planet.

Naturally, I am not offering a brick-and-mortar step-by-step approach with details about how to manage the proposed new system. I leave that to more qualified experts to handle the details. Moreover, I have opted to publish my proposed solution to overhaul our present economic system in a book form to preserve its identity and existence and to encourage my fellow humans to read it. Furthermore, I have also taken the liberty to express my views on other subjects that shape our day-to-day living and offer some suggestions to improve the prevailing system that merit consideration. I have listed these topics under the table of contents. Of course, it is up to us collectively to pass judgments on their merit.

In any event, the salient question that we should ask ourselves is whether it is justifiable and compelling to let an artificial, compulsory, unsustainable, and dreadful income-tax system hold the key to our survival.

The Inspiration

The spark, which ignited my thinking to tackle the subject of economics overhaul, sprang on me unexpectedly one day while strolling in the woods. As I walked, my attention was suddenly drawn to my right side, where I saw a family of deer vigorously chewing what Mother Nature had offered them. As I stopped to enjoy looking at this marvelous picture, the elderly of the group stopped eating, advanced a few paces toward me, and began to stare at me intensely. I interpreted his look as telling me, "What are you looking at? Get moving and let us enjoy our meal for free, compliments of Mother Nature."

As I resumed movement, I thought to myself how magnificent this was and how Mother Nature generously provides sustenance to the animal kingdom without asking for anything in return. Comparing us supposedly thinking humans with the animal kingdom, how wonderful it is that animals can eat what they want and when they want without paying anything in return. Mother Nature never asks them to pay for what they consume, whereas for us supposedly smart Homo Sapiens, we must have money to eat. So for those of us who don't have it can be deprived of Mother Nature's life-sustaining needs.

Unquestionably, animals have one serious drawback: the large can eat the small, and the strong can dominate and consume the weak. Humans, on the other hand, have, in the passage of time, created and lived with the "have and the have not" status. So my on-and-off thinking about our economic life led me to dig deep for the roots of our economic inequality and how the quantity of money became the supreme arbiter that rules our life on our precious planet.

Despite my limited artistic ability to recreate what I had seen, I was able to express it with oil on canvas for your eyes to see. And here it comes:

What Is Wrong With Our Present Economic System?

To begin with, most of us live totally engrossed by our daily routines and needs to make a living, and that limits our thinking horizon to look beyond our noses and immediate scope of vision. Thus, we are compelled to follow the stream of our daily activities and have no time or appetite for questioning the prevailing economic system and examining alternatives to it.

Since the beginning of time, in the process of economic evolution and embracing the feeble income-tax system, we have created crippling barriers and shackles and placing a noose around our necks that we keep on tightening it as we move along while adhering to its unjustifiable requirements.

As a unique species living on a wonderful planet in a vast universe which is virtually our home, we have attained a relatively advanced status in the evolution process. Mother

Nature has endowed us with perception and intelligence and the ability to learn, think, reason, observe, and even predict what lies ahead for us in the future. Granted, some of us have superior native ability and intelligence; nevertheless, it is not that hard for the rest of us to recognize that given the trend of job losses that would undoubtedly reduce the collections of income-taxes that would unquestionably result in having insufficient dollars in the treasury to fulfill our needs, we will have to find a way to get the dollars to fill in the shortfall. Let's not forget that we are already living under a considerable imbalance of income and expense and swimming in debt.

On the spending side of the equation, the numbers are increasing steadily because of population growth. The need to restoring neglected vital projects, such as rebuilding our deteriorating armed forces, cannot be fulfilled because of budget restraints. It is undeniable that our infrastructure is in dire need of uplifting. Our healthcare system is atrocious. Our education standards are lagging. So given such a situation which we are in, staying the course, our train would be derailed and head towards falling off the cliff. Hence, it is absolutely imperative to change course.

Quite obviously, the logical solution under our existing economic system will have to be increasing taxes, insanely borrowing more money or living with what we have, and let nature take its course and let the chips fall where they may. We should not let this destiny happen if it could be avoided.

Borrowing the money as a collective society and creating debt within the present economic frame is not the right answer to our economic needs. As of the start of 2017, the national debt is about to climb above a staggering high of $20 trillion. Natural disasters, wars, and recessions can further diminish government savings if any, and push us deeper into red ink. The income- tax burden is disproportionately falling on the few high earners. As tax payers, one half of us as a group, pay incredibly less than 3% of the total collected taxes. The other 50% pays more than 97% of the tax burden. The top 10% of taxpayers pays over 70%, the top 5% pays over 58% and the top 1% pays over 36%. Clearly, low earners and the unemployed are tipping the scale. This picture does not look well for the future of the country. Clearly, increasing the tax burden on those already paying the most is not only unjust but also would not make much of a dent in the ocean- deep national debt.

Let us recognize first of all that our economic system is totally artificial, hurled on humanity in the passage of time, to which we are compelled to follow to live in our society. It is totally inconsistent with the natural creation process.

Humans began using money about 2,500 years ago. It evolved out of deeply rooted customs of using other forms of money for bartering purposes, such as cattle, cowrie shells, whale's teeth, and ornamental jewelry. Granted, the use of money is justifiable as a measuring tool for exchanging goods and services with one and another and for accumulating wealth by each of us individually. Thus, as individuals, we have got to have money upfront to acquire goods and services. But unjustifiably, this practice had spilled over to the other side, making it also imperative, under our existing economic system, to have the needed money available upfront when acting as a group for the benefit of all of us to attend to humanity's vital needs. So here is where the problem lies—acting as individuals for our personal benefit versus acting collectively for the benefits of all of us.

Clearly and without doubt, for a mass population of humans living together in one country—never mind on one planet—not having enough money as a group to meet our vital needs can vastly impede our progress and forward movement in science, health maintenance, and care of our sagging infrastructure. It would rob us of discoveries of better sources of energy. Science helps us to unlock the secrets of nature and can propel us forward when new discoveries are made. Therefore, we must solve this problem if we want to live to see the future.

According to a study by the Dallas Federal Reserve Bank, the 2007–2009 financial crisis had cost the nation over $14 trillion dollars, which is equivalent to a one-year economic output, and its effect is still with us. This was followed by a moderate recovery and a litany of other economic effects. Under our existing economic system, it is very difficult to recover from such a gap, and as interest rates move higher, the federal debt will swell further.

There are valid arguments that the recession caused by the real-estate bust could have been avoided or at least lessened if we had acted differently. Under our economic system, banks are required to carry their real-estate assets on their balance sheet "marked to market"—this means at current market value, subjected to supply and demand.

In reality, however, the intrinsic value of the quantity of matter (land, material, and structure) did not change. The commodity involved here is not perishable, and its steep decline of prices due to oversold market had to be temporary. Since home mortgages are closely tied to the prevailing market value of the homes, the application of "mark to market" by banks to their real-estate business drove some banks unnecessarily to near insolvency and pushed mortgage loans to submerge under water. If banks were allowed to carry these assets on their balance sheets at, let's say, 10% below their original appraised value, much of the hardships could have been averted.

Let us not forget that Mother Nature is the unconditional sole provider to all there is. She will never ask us for money upfront to harness her powers to produce what we need regardless of how much money there is in the treasury. When Adam and Eve first walked the earth, they had no job and no savings except what the planet Earth yielded freely.

Our economy is now dependent on how much money we can collect through taxes. The prevailing inner dynamics call for increased spending due to the population growth on one side. But on the other side, the dynamics are pushing us in the opposite direction, that of a declining job market. So to fill the gap, we desperately need to increase taxes, thereby making the situation worse. In reality, we need to increase jobs first in order to beef up our tax revenues. Clearly, staying on this track our train will fall off the cliff.

Objectives

Our objectives should be directed toward two goals. The first is to replace our existing economic system with a more accommodating and a realistic plan, geared toward fostering prosperity and improving the quality of life for all of us. Our economic system should be consistent with our current status in the natural creation process and our level of civilization to fulfill our needs for the present and the future. The second is to consider how to prepare people for the future's new mode of living with much idle time at hand as technology will spare us most of the time-consuming labor work.

For the immediate future, given the current status of our economics and the underlying dynamics in play, which will shape our future, it is most important now, as I said earlier, to trumpet a wake-up call to fellow humans to stress that our existing economic system is flawed, unnecessarily impeding the quality of life across the land, and can lead us to an ominous future. Hence, we must fix this damaging economic system as soon as possible without fail. The stakes are very high.

First of all, whatever we do should be based on the one overriding principle that humanity's well-being should come first, and safeguarding it should stand in the forefront of our objectives in adopting a new system. Money should not stand in the way. At present, we have a system which is impeding our quality of life and totally disregarding our well-being instead of fostering the fulfillments of our needs. Clearly, we are enslaved by it.

Therefore, what we need is a system that serves us and not us serving it. I once read that on one clear sunny day, Jesus was observed toiling in the garden on the Sabbath.

He was asked, "Are you not violating the Sabbath?"

To that, he replied, "Remember, the Sabbath was made for man, and man was not made for the Sabbath."

I thought this was a fittingly realistic and marvelous answer. So we need to put in place an economic system that would serve us and enable us to live among educated and healthy people.

Accordingly, our objective is first to expose the pitfalls of our present economic system, and that it should be replaced with a new system in which we can provide a working and realistic solution to attend to society's needs and to remove the misery that comes with it. To accomplish this objective, we should abide by nature's law of cause and effect, and create the cause and weave the fabric that would result in what we want to safeguard humanity's well-being and provide ready access to free healthcare and free education at all levels. All of us should have roofs over our heads and be able to feed our families without concern about having the cursed money.

Knowing that we humans have to work to earn our keep, consequently, our primary efforts should be focused on creating jobs and dealing with their ongoing disappearances. Undoubtedly, the treasury will have to find the source of money to finance these projects in full. This will be a tough call.

Naturally, in order to achieve our goals, we need to have a planned economy which adjusts to the needs of society in a well-managed manner to ensure that all able bodies do their share.

I wholeheartedly believe that by changing our economic system, we can spare ourselves from all the ravaging and avoidable suffering from the economic upheavals caused by depressions, recessions, unemployment, inflation, bursting market bubbles, the financial miscalculation incurred by the few which hurls calamities on the masses, and the inability of people to afford food, shelter, and healthcare.

Most importantly, such a plan must provide incentives for people to the extent of their ability to excel and be self-sufficient, productive, and creative, and be able to contribute to the nation's economic well-being, and, furthermore, allowing individuals to retain their hard-earned wealth and for the don't-haves to accumulate some wealth. By eliminating these economic hardships, we will have a healthy and more educated and productive society.

Moreover, under nature's rule of cause and effect, crime will have a diminished driving force behind it. People are the country's best assets. They represent a reservoir of talent and creativity. With the launching of the Internet, new jobs have been created, but many jobs have and are being eliminated constantly. So we must plan for the future, and find ways to help the unemployed, and train them for suitable lines of work to regain their livelihood and dignity.

Humans by nature are inherently like to work and not sit idle. Just look at the long lines of the unemployed applying for work when it's available. But yes, there may be some who would rather loaf if they could find ready and easy means of support. It is within our reach to stop that by eliminating food stamps and replacing it with training and employing idle people except for the sick and the disabled.

So in short, our primary objective is to see to it that no human should be deprived of food, shelter, healthcare, and education because of not having money available upfront. This does not mean opening the safe to give money away freely but to do it by creating jobs and training the idles.

Our sagging infrastructure needs much upgrading, and we must do what's necessary regardless of how much money there is in the treasury. It will be self-evident that attending to our needs as a group collectively should not depend on what is in the treasury's purse. Our unemployment is high.

Lack of funds leaves us in a freezing position, and in fact, unemployment places a heavy burden on our debt under the present economic system.

Now ask yourself, if we could find a source to get the funds to build bridges and roads and do whatever is needed to strengthen the infrastructure, would that virtually put many of the idles to work, reduce our debt, and generate wealth for workers? Of course it would. The burden of the unemployed would be lifted.

Research in physics, biology, and all sciences must be pursued vigorously to unleash the powers of Mother Nature and open the floodgates of prosperity across the land. Just imagine the benefits of harnessing the unlimited and mighty power of hydrogen fusion to give ourselves light.

Lack of money has led us to dangerously cut NASA's wings and seriously curtail highly beneficial programs to explore outer space, go back to the moon, and travel to Mars and beyond. So we need to have an economic system that would not stop us from exploring outer space and reaching for the stars.

In any event, unlocking the secrets of nature is humanities best ally to propel us forward into the future, and we must put scientific research and developments in the forefront of our priorities and not cripple it by the lack of the almighty dollar and the artificial, useless budgets. We need to appoint a deep-thinking team of the best minds among us to chart our future and deal with job losses for many of us, caused by technology's rapid advancements.

Let us take an example of how the onset of the Internet has initiated a trend for eliminating jobs. Buying goods online has considerably shrunk the working sales force as a result of closing stores, with no stopping in sight. What is coming up on the horizon is the next job killer, and that is robotics. These now unthinking human imitations are being gradually perfected and phased into the service industry. Robots, in the eyes of the employers, do not need vacations, ongoing healthcare, retirement benefits, or pay to do the work, and in time, they will be able to fill many jobs, pushing some of us out the door. So let's not forget that artificial intelligence in technology can be another unrestrained job killer to contend with.

Most importantly, these technology advancements are creating inner dynamics which promote job losses. On one hand, we have business entities that are constantly attempting to find new ways to cut costs and beef up the bottom line. So this makes them eager to adopt the new technology if it can reduce the head count. On the other hand, new technology is surfacing every day and is providing the helping hands to cut jobs. For example, robots are already perfected to flip hamburgers very efficiently with precision while sensing the cooking status of the meat. Can you imagine how many workers could lose their jobs to these robots?

Here is another one. The military has pursued an objective to build trucks that can drive themselves, justifiably to save solders' lives in the battlefields. This will eventually, without a question, spill over to the private sector. So what is going to happen to all those truck drivers now on the highways, moving cargo from one city to another? Just imagine how much money can be saved by business entities when switching to self-driven trucks—very considerable. Besides their wages, there is substantial healthcare and pension costs. Therefore, it is imperative—the sooner, the better—to have a plan for retraining workers to do other work before the age of robotics will fully take hold.

So without doubt, we need to put in place a new sweeping and simple economic structure that can wipe out poverty, and cure the debacles of the past, create harmony and a healthy society, and, with that, explore the feasibility of eliminating the feeble, burdensome, and complicated income-tax system and closing the doors of the Internal Revenue System.

With respect to the second part of our objectives, which should be focused upon, as I stated earlier, how to fill the idle time as a result of that many of us will not be working, it is important to keep in mind that evolution does not progress on the same level among us. Some of us can embrace art, music, and science to fill our spare time. For those who have no inclination for such hobbies, we will have to plan for suitable engagements to avoid the onset of mischievous behavior caused by idleness and boredom. The proposed formation of the Steering Seven Group should lend a hand in finding solutions to such a troubling situation.

How Did We Get Where We Are?

In the beginning when humans walked on the earth, understandably, to survive, they had to find or build shelter, hunt, and fish, and create all the necessities of life. You could perform all these tasks yourself, but that may not be possible or practical. As a result, this led to a swapping bartering system. You fish, and I farm, and we exchange what we have with each other, thereby swapping goods and services and that brought about a bartering system.

As the circle widened to make the system work more efficiently, a unit of value had to be invented, and money was born. As a result, humans became obsessed with money. So to eat, you must have money or go hungry.

Naturally, for a group of people to live together, villages, towns, cities, and nations surfaced on the globe. Vital services to benefit all people became necessary, such as building roads and having armies, police protection, and judges to resolve disputes and enact laws to foster harmonious living with one and another to serve the collective needs of the masses. This brought about appointing government officials to carry out these tasks. And that, of course, need money. To get it, the cursed income-tax system became the law of the land.

The inability of governments to pair taxes with spending put us into debt. The increase in the short fall, which could be the result of war and natural disasters, led to increasing taxes. To manipulate the tax system, it is often used as a carrot to stimulate business to help boost our economy. Depending on the judgments of government officials, some vital services may at times be impaired.

Without having the precious money in hand, our progress in research and developments, space exploration, and other vital works would be crippled. The contribution of poor management would sink us further into debt and tighten the economic noose on humanity's neck. Economically, we find ourselves on a sailboat with little power at the mercy of the waves and the wind. Furthermore, we live under the danger of being hit by asteroids and meteors that could, at any time, wipe us out in one blow. Money availability restrains our efforts to develop effective means to destroy or divert these dangerous intruders.

The Basics: Our Economic System Should Be Consistent With The Laws Of Nature

Let's you and I walk through time, starting with the creation process, and know where we are and our place in our vast universe.

I'm bringing up the subject of creation and the forces of nature because it is one of the most important pillars on which we can and should build our economic system. Also, in my view, some basic knowledge about the laws of nature and how our universe was created and how it works should be understood by every human and kept in prospective in our daily living to maintain harmony with the natural forces. After all, the universe is our home.

Much to our good fortune today, there is a wealth of scientific knowledge about the creation of the universe that has been tested and validated. The Internet contains a sea of freely accessible information for us to tap. Scientists tell us the creation of the Universe is such an ingenious, beautiful, and sophisticated work, that it is almost impossible to comprehend. Yet the universe is clearly a reality that exists for us, and we should attempt to learn the basics. The reluctance to do so under the pretext "that I am not good at math and physics" is self-proclaimed that may not be true.

The book of Genesis begins with "In the beginning, God created the heaven and the earth. And the earth was without form and void, and darkness was upon the face of the deep."

Scientists agree that the universe was created from, you can say, nothingness. Following the big bang, the forces of nature went to work, starting with a ray of light (a photon). Particles teamed together to create electrons, neutrons, and other subatomic particles, leading to atoms of hydrogen, oxygen, carbon, and others. As we all know, two atoms of hydrogen and one of oxygen form the water we drink.

Then gravity exerted its force to squeeze and fuse the clouds of hydrogen atoms, igniting them to provide fuel for the shining stars and spouting helium behind as ashes. The process went on to create galaxies and planets, and then life sprang out. It is predicted that eventually, our sun will exhaust its fuel and die out. New stars such as our sun will be born. It is interesting to know that the reason for the heavenly objects, such as the planets and the moons, to be round is because gravity pulls in equal force from all directions.

The Basics: Our Economic System Should Be Consistent With The Laws Of Nature

The point I am attempting to demonstrate is that life is an ongoing cycles of creation and dying out. Trees grow and flourish. The leaves wither out and dissolve, followed by new growth. Fruits are materialized to be consumed or rotted out and returned back to the soil if not eaten. When consumed, it will also return to the soil in another form. Water evaporates only to rise and condense into clouds and come down as rain.

Animals and humans are born and eventually die. Scientists tell us that it is important to understand and keep in mind that the sum total of energy in our universe remains the same. So whatever we harness from Mother Nature for our use is returnable to Mother Nature. Clearly then, Mother Nature is the true sustainer of life and not the quantity of money that we have or that we don't have. So in the process of reforming matter by building bridges and roads, nothing is lost that needs to be restored. The availability of money should have no place in this process.

To imagine the scope of our universe. We live on a planet which is part of a vast universe, harboring more than 100 billion galaxies. In our galaxy alone, there are over 100 billion stars. So our planet is like a speck on a mountain of sand. Research is being done to confirm the theory that our universe is one of many.

The four fundamental forces of nature that powers everything are gravity, electromagnetism, the weak nuclear force, and the strong nuclear force. Gravity holds the solar system together and keeps us anchored to the ground. The electromagnetic force gives us light to brighten our cities, and energizes our engines, and powers our computers and lasers. The strong and weak nuclear forces hold the nucleus of the atom together.

If we look at our bodies, by mass, we are composed of about 47 to 60% water, depending on how lean one is. The rest is fat and protein. By elements, 61% oxygen, 23% carbon, and 10% hydrogen. The rest are nitrogen, sulfur, sodium, potassium, and others.

Let's start by putting reality in prospective. The laws of nature govern all that there is across the board. Most importantly, under the laws of thermodynamics, the amount of matter and energy in the universe is constant. So whatever we can harness and use from our natural resources will not be lost. We are born with nothing and will eventually depart with nothing, regardless of how much wealth we have. Whatever we own, from the clothes we wear to the buildings we live in, to the food we eat, and the water we drink, to the air we breathe, and the skin on our bodies all are the products of Mother Nature. I think we know all of that.

There is an urge in us for charity. Our universe exudes with spiritual feeling. The laws of cause and effect are paramount and basic and can bring about desired or unwanted changes. So clearly, whatever happens, there is a cause behind it. As a society, we have the power of concentration to act collectively. It is not difficult for us to look far beyond the horizon and plan for the future.

Understandably, we live mostly overburdened with our pursuit to earn our daily living, and therefore, we get distracted, and our eyes are not on the ball to pay attention to what lies ahead. Those of us who are specialized in what they do are focused on their fields of specialties: education, medicine, finance, electronics, and others. Our elected officials are deeply concerned about getting reelected and defending strengthening their parties. Safeguarding the party's interest may at times be placed above the interest of the country as a whole. At most, scientists are the ones who often sound the alarm about the dangers ahead. So our ship is mostly left to drift with the wind.

But the truth is that we do have the intelligence to recognize that not having the money in the treasury should not stop us from forging forward in building and researching to move ahead. As individuals, we don't ask or want to know how much money is in the treasury's purse to work for the government as long as we get paid.

To go a step further in understanding the basics which govern our daily living, as humans to do labor in all aspects of life and creative thinking, our bodies require fuel. To this end, our bodies extract energy from ingested food. Carbohydrates, fats, and proteins in the food we eat are our potential fuel source. They all ultimately yield water, carbon dioxide, and a chemical energy called

Adenosine Triphosphate (ATP). The ATP molecules are high-energy compounds or batteries that store energy for us to use. And here we go again; our principal supplier of food is Mother Nature, with no charge.

Let's take, for example, the cost of the food we eat. It consists of the farmer's labor and land acquisition, plus the machinery acquired for farming, the seeds, the packaging, the transportation, and any other means of putting the end product on the shelves—plus profit if any. These elements are usually paid for by the private sector. The products itself fruits, vegetables, and whatever the land can yield plus the energy used by labor—are given to us by Mother Nature for free. This is the essential element in the creation process. Given these simple and obvious facts, the quantity of money can still stand in the way of how much food we can produce, and we should not let this be the case. So one more time, we need to find a way to remove this restriction to brighten our future.

We Are Not Genetically Created Equal

If we were created equal, not likely there would be big financial gaps among the people, and there will be no such a thing as rich and poor. Under the U.S. Declaration of Independence, we all have equal rights to life, liberty, and the pursuit of happiness. So the road is widely open to all of us to succeed and accumulate wealth on our own. It seems evident that this diversity in our capabilities had to be part of the creation process, to promote our survival and to balance the fulfillment of humanity's needs. Thus, some of us would prefer to work with their hands as carpenters, plumbers, builders and do other manual work. Others may wish to be fisherman or farmers. Then there are those who have creative ability and those who could take on other professions, such as teaching or embracing the medical or the scientific fields. Apparently, such a design helps us to move forward by providing a variety of abilities to fulfill all aspects of our needs and improve the quality of life on the planet.

It is undisputable that that we are not created genetically the same. It is in front of our eyes, to see the endless varieties in looks and in native abilities. Of course, this has nothing to do with race, ethnicity, religion, nationality, or any other origins. So this has to be nature's design. The same rule applies to the animal kingdom and the foods that we eat. For an example, there are about 340 breeds of dogs and 80 to 100 breeds of cats. In the fruits category, can you believe it—? Worldwide, there are about 7,500 varieties of apples, the staggering number of varieties of mushrooms, scientist claim, can reach 140,000. I can go on without limit.

So until we can master genetic alterations, we must accept who we are as we are and not demand to be someone else. As we can readily observe, in the creation process, the gifts of nature range from strength and physical ability levels of perceptions to observe and recognize what exists. Some of us are creative artistically oriented inventors in depth thinkers, and others may have leadership qualities. Some of us may grow tall or short. Some are strongly built, more muscular than others, and can easily carry heavy objects. This would enable such humans to become very rich athletes. For those of us who are more perceptive and smarter than others are apt to be scientists, doctors, artists, or even leaders. Let us not forget that there are those who possess better looks, giving them a leg upon to success over the rest of us. But most importantly, there are some of us who are smart enough to find ways to take advantage of our existing economic system, to forge ahead and acquire wealth and prosper, leaving others behind and thus resulting in those who have and those who have not.

Such economic inequality can happen because in our free society, we all have, as stated earlier, equal rights to life, liberty, and the pursuit of happiness and can forge ahead on our own. Hence, under such a climate, it would not be in the best interest of society as a whole, under the pretext of encouragement, to elevate people and put them in positions to which they are not the best suited and capable.

With recognition to this reality, we should provide the guidance, education, and training to boost the have-nots and make them self-sufficient. Moreover, it is important that the have-nots should not begrudge the successful and demand equal footings financially. It should be recognized that for this group, if society would provide free education, healthcare, and other help to acquire skills, they should be grateful and should attempt to climb the ladder of success on their own. Therefore, to maintain harmony among us, we must consider this reality of the creation process when forming our economic system. We should lend a helping hand to those who need it. Most importantly, we must find ways to provide free healthcare and education openly to all of us equally without pay.

History is an incredible witness. Just think—who among us can say he or she is created equal to, take for example, the scientists, the artists, the writers, and leaders such as Leonardo da Vinci, Isaac Newton, Ludwig van Beethoven,

Wolfgang Amadeus Mozart, Albert Einstein, and many other iconic figures that influenced our world? Moreover, it is no secret that much of the world's problems emanate from the haves and have-nots and from religious bigotry. Poor people have a greater need to cling to religion, thereby intensifying the rifts among the inhabitants of the land. So we must make every effort to lift up those trailing behind economically.

Just think of it. When Isaac Newton, born premature and a small human, discovered gravity, he opened the door to the Industrial Revolution and the creation of the steam engine, which powered locomotives. The second leap forward came when Thomas Edison, with the help of Michael Faraday and James Clerk Maxwell, discovered and harnessed electricity and magnetism and declared, "Let there be light." Our cities became bright throughout the night and gave power to our appliances. Then ushered the electronic revolution, giving us many scientific wonders. Our next leap forward was understanding nuclear forces.

When that "lazy dog" Albert Einstein, as one of his teachers called him, came up with his famous equation—$E=mc^2$ square—we split the atom to produce the awesome atomic energy. And today, with the understanding of the quantum theory and dealing with the subatomic world, we have lasers, transistors, and digital jargon. This theory is also helping scientists to unlock the secrets of the DNA molecules.

Therefore, unlike us individuals, who must have money in our pockets to attend to our personal needs, for a society as a whole, it should not be the same. We must find a way for not letting the unavailability of dollars stand in the way of scientific research and discoveries that could inhibit our progress in unlocking the secrets of nature to discover new ways to safeguard and improve the quality of living on our planet.

Just ask yourself, what price can you put on these scientific breakthroughs? How much can we gain by identifying and fixing the genetic material responsible for humanity's serious ailments? The cost of healthcare would plummet to the ground, and humanities will be spared from the agony of many diseases. Now think of it—what would happen if we succeeded in harnessing the power of fusion? A bucket of water would yield energy equivalent to millions of gallons of petroleum.

Let us not forget and keep in mind that the lack of funds has led our government, most unwisely, to curtail and limit NASA's (The National Aeronautics and Space Administration) activities, and not recognizing that our most serious source of danger is what's lurking around us in outer space. Just ask yourself what would happen if a sizable meteor or an asteroid hit one of our large and thickly populated cities—such as New York, Los Angeles, or Chicago—and kills all of its inhabitants.? We will be screaming to kingdom come to intensify NASA's tracking activities of these intruders and to develop effective means to destroy or divert them away from our planet. In fact, it might even be too late for all of us. We will simply follow the path of extinction of the dinosaurs.

What Is Wealth?

We all know that wealth basically includes cash (money), investments in financial instruments, buildings, land, jewelry, and other marketable objects.

Let's take a look at money. The *Merriam–Webster Dictionary* defines *money* as "anything that serves as a common medium of exchange in trade as coin or notes." Money can be anything created and accepted by a society as a tool and common yardstick for exchanging goods and services and payment of debts. Every country has its own system of coins and paper money. Thus, money represents the quantity of units of value, available for acquiring goods and services subject to current market rates. Hence, its value could deteriorate by inflation when held as money over a period of time, causing its purchasing power for goods and services to go down, while its rate of exchange with foreign currencies can also fluctuate.

But for a society, encompassing a group of people living together, regrettably, the availability of money has taken over to become the ruler of life, impeding forward movement and progress on the planet. Over the last 10,000 years, the material form of money has changed considerably—from cattle and cowrie shells to today's electronic currency.

As stated earlier, virtually, the need for inventing money was to facilitate bartering. In the beginning, humans wanted to exchange goods with one another. Let's say, for example, you are an avid fisherman. Your neighbor happens to grow chickens and eggs. You arrange to swap with him fish for some chickens and eggs in return.

So from the beginning, people swapped items of value. Many things have been exchanged in the marketplace, among them livestock, sacks of cereal grain from which the Israeli Shekel was derived, tea, tobacco, and other things of use. Some attractive items such as cowrie shells or beads were exchanged for more useful commodities, such as precious metals from which early coins were made. However, barter was not practical when you wanted to obtain certain goods from a producer that does not want what you have. This created problems for people, for which the solution was money.

Money was born about 2,500 years ago. The first mintage of coins showed up in the sixth century BC. Metal money and coins were used in 1000 BC. Modern coinage came aboard in 500 BC, with leather money in about 118 BC. In 800 to 900 AD it was the nose. You probably heard the phrase "You will pay through the nose." This comes from

Danes in Ireland, who slit the noses of those who were remiss in paying the Danish poll tax.

In 1816, the gold standard was instituted but that was ended in 1930. The beginning of the end of the gold standard came about in the massive depression of the 1930. In the United States, the gold standard was revised, and the price of gold was devalued. The British and international gold standard soon ended, creating complexities of international monetary regulation. Today currency continues to change and develop, as evidenced by the new $100 U.S. Ben Franklin bill. But most of our transactions take place electronically, without exchanging physical money.

It is quite obvious and absolutely truthful to say that money as part of our wealth is merely refers to how much credit we have available at hand for exchanging goods and services for us as individuals. It is simply a yardstick of that quantity available for bartering purposes. Obviously, we all need it to pay for our needs to live. But there is no compelling reason to apply the same rule when acting as a society and unnecessarily hold ourselves back from forging ahead to do what we need to do.

Inflation

As we all know, inflation occurs when the prices of goods and services increase over time. Inflation cannot be measured by an increase in the cost of one product or service or even several products or services. Rather, inflation is a general increase in the overall price level of the goods and services in the economy. Over the years, inflation has substantially increased the cost of goods and services unrealistically and thereby boosted the monetary values of wealth. Thus, we can say that, indeed, part of our wealth comes from inflation. Wages and costs of living drive each other up. When the cost of living goes up, it requires more income to make ends meet. A boost in income creates a higher demand for goods and services, pushing prices higher, and so inflation is unabated. Here are some examples of the magnitude of inflation.

In 1950, the cost of a subway ride in New York City was just a dime. Today it's $3, thirtyfold. At the same time span, the cost of buying the New York Times newspaper jumped fiftyfold form a nickel to $2.50. So realistically, wealth equals inflation plus invested money with its diminished value, plus tangible assets—e.g., land, buildings plus stocks and bonds, which are subject to price change, the value of all of which is influenced by inflation.

So in theory, inflation could do no harm as long as income rises proportionately to meet the higher cost of living on a relative basis. But in practice, inflation can be distressing to those living on fixed income and certainly widening the gap between the haves and the have-nots and creating difficulties for people to make ends meet. The accumulated nest egg of the wealthy invested in other than cash would naturally rise.

James Smart And Timothy Slim

I am writing this story, which is based on facts, to demonstrate how wealth can accumulate by some of us and denied to others.

James Smart and Tim Slim were close friends and grew up together. Both worked for the same company, but James started working two years before Tim. As a result, James was able to put money aside. Within five years, James had $10,000 dollars in his nest egg, while Tim had no savings. The town they lived in was expanding rapidly, so new homes were being constructed to accommodate newcomers. James and Tim decided to move to these new homes as neighbors. James used his $10,000 savings as a down payment and bought the house for $30,000. Tim had no money on the side, so his only option was renting. Five years later, both were married; James had two children, but Tim got three. As time passed by, James continued his habit of putting some money aside, while Tim's higher living expenses limited his ability to save.

One day, in December of 1974, James eyes spotted a pile of empty bottles of Coca-Cola in the kitchen which they had consumed. He was struck with the idea that most likely, other people are doing the same thing and drinking this beverage. He asked himself, why not get a piece of the action? So when he got his year-end bonus, he went out and bought himself 20 shares of Coke at the price of $53 per share.

At the end of December of 2012, 38 years later, James's mortgage on his house was fully paid, and he owned his house free and clear. The value of his house has appreciated 30 times to $900,000. His 20 shares of Coke were split six times since he bought them, increasing the number of shares to 960, worth $38,400. He was tempted to cash in his stock, but when he learned that he would have to share his profit with Uncle Sam by paying taxes, he was discouraged. So James's assets, the house, and the stock had appreciated in value and were worth $938,000, while his neighbor Tim had nothing to brag about.

At this point, we are seeing the roll of money and how savings and investments boosted by inflation can be that catalyst for creating wealth for ourselves individually and how the haves and the have-nots emerge. The values used here are real, consistent with the prevailing market and the time of occurrence.

As shown here, when we examine wealth deeply, we find that most of it is inflation and has no real intrinsic value.

Jim Smart's $30,000 house jumped in price to $900,000. Where did that wealth come from? The building material from which the house was constructed had basically remained the same, having the same mass, representing the same amount of energy spent to build it. So wealth is indeed mostly artificial, created by inflation in the costs of material and labor. It is considered wealth simply because we all agree and accept it collectively that it has bartering value at current higher market prices.

This is a typical example illustrating how the market dynamics work. Clearly, wealth creates more wealth when held in marketable material and not in cash. This could easily widen the gap further between the haves and have-nots.

Overhauling The System

As a group of a supposedly civilized, intelligent people, it is time to recognize that money was not intended to dictate and shape humanity's life, our future, and well-being. Having defined the basic realities to use as pillars upon which we should build a new economic structure, which may appear to be vastly outlandish to some of us, let's start by reviewing them.

The universe was created from nothingness. So we can say there is nothing in everything and everything in nothing. Nevertheless, we are here on a planet that supplies all of our needs without asking us for anything in return. We simply need to harvest her resources in a well-planned manner. Under nature's law of thermodynamics, scientists tell us that the amount of matter and energy in the universe remains constant. It merely changes from one form to another. This means that whatever we take from Mother Nature will not diminish her capacity. All that we eat, drink, wear, and build, including our bodies, are provided by Mother Nature and will return to her.

We are not genetically created equal. This is important to consider in our economics planning. Therefore, some of us might not be able to compete on equal footing with others and may lag behind economically, the result of which—and what we now have—is not only the haves and the have-nots but also the inability to get jobs to earn a healthy and comfortable living.

Nature's cause-and-effect forces could lead deprived people to steal and commit crimes. Therefore, it is vital and in the best interest of all the inhabitants of the land to give a hand to those who lag behind, most importantly not supporting them by draining wealth from the wealthy and the successful but by training them to work in suitable jobs to earn a decent living and by ensuring that education and healthcare are provided equally to all of us without pay.

Most importantly, we must understand that the role of money in our life is nothing more than a representation of the units of value that we have earned and saved for our benefit to use for bartering purposes. It is recognized and accepted, more or less, by all of us as a credit for what we have earned from work and other income, issued by the central government to the citizens for acquiring goods and services and for saving and investing for the future. Also equally important to know that in a substantial part, wealth is mostly created from nothingness, namely, inflation. So consistent with what we have been doing, as individuals, we need to earn our living and live by our means, subject to how much money we have or for what we can borrow.

But such availability of money should not be binding for us collectively as a society. This is where our economic problems are coming from. And so by carefully examining our economic structure, there can be no doubt that for us individuals money remains the ruler of our life, and we need to have it first before we can acquire the necessities and luxuries of life. But it is entirely unjustifiable, and there is absolutely no valid reason that we, the people living on a small planet in a vast universe, be stopped from teaming up together collectively to authorize our representative government to attend to our needs as a group to give credits in the form of dollars to those engaged to do the necessary work without reliance on the feeble income-tax money to be collected.

Naturally, there should be no limitation on the amounts of dollars that can be given as credits for work done, simply because it is authorized by all of us and carries the full faith and credit of the U.S. government, and that is us, the citizens. It need not be backed by gold or silver or any other articles of value as long as we all recognize, guarantee, and accept its worthiness as guaranteed by all of us collectively. This will be consistent with the current status of our money today. However, we must have strict controls to prevent unjustifiable spending and corruption.

Therefore, under this tenet, we can fund and provide free healthcare and education to all, and do whatever is necessary to safeguard life, build our infrastructure, protect our environment, and do all we can in the scientific research arena to unlock the secrets of Mother Nature, where humanities future lies.

By removing our reliance, when acting as a group, on the limited income-tax system and instead authorizing our representative government to attend to our needs on all fronts and, of course, to spend whatever it takes to attain our objectives, we can do whatever we need to do. Indeed, we will be opening the floodgates of prosperity. We can provide ourselves with superior free healthcare and all levels of education. Let's face it—if we stay the course and let our future be dependent on the feeble income-tax system and let it hold us hostage, impeding our forward movement because we do not have enough money in the Treasury to move ahead on our vital needs, we will be unnecessarily hurting ourselves.

Therefore, to cure our economic illness, we have to overhaul the present economic system by discontinuing our reliance on the limited amount of money collected through income-tax. Instead, we the people should collectively empower our representative government to issue credits in the form of dollars to pay for attending to our vital needs without limitations. It is crystal clear that if we continue to depend and limit our spending to the collection of income-tax, that will inescapably lead us to disastrous consequences.

However, it is not hard to predict that there will be some among us, particularly economists, who may find this proposition shocking and unacceptable. But let us face it. At the rate we are going, jobs will continue to dry up, thereby not only reducing tax revenues but also requiring more unemployment insurance costs. Technology will further eat up most of what's left in jobs and can be further devastating when robots populate the land. Remember, these hardworking dummies don't need healthcare, retirement pay, education, or any living wages, thus increasing their appeal to the business world for beefing up the bottom line.

In removing money availability from the front line as a condition to do what's needed collectively as a society, we will be in tune with the laws of nature under which mother earth and her home universe, which is now and always is the real provider of life's needs for humans and animals alike. So whatever we take from mother earth is replenishable, but that must be pursued intelligently with attention to resources, locations, and capacities. Food-production capacity must always exceed consumption needs.

And so to reiterate that the basic economic tenant for overhauling our economic system is first, as individuals, we must continue to live by our means from the amounts of money we earn and save and from any wealth that we may have accumulated over time. As for all of us collectively, there is no valid reason for us to let money stonewall our efforts to do what is necessary to maintain a decent living for all. That should also include all aspects of life, such as healthcare, education, security, research and development, building infrastructure, etc. And so when acting collectively as a group, money availability should not decide for us on what we deem vital for us to do. Our government, as empowered by us collectively, can issue all the dollars needed to get the job done.

Having been conditioned to living under a system which places money as the source from which all things come, some readers and economists most likely will object and raise the question; if we spend all that needed money freely without any limitation to attend to our vital needs, how will this money be eventually paid back? Are we creating a heavy burden on our future generations? The answer to that is absolutely no; it does not have to come from any place and be paid back. Furthermore, we are not creating a burden on our future generation, and here is why:

First, we are not borrowing the money from anyone that would require paying it back. What we are realistically doing under nature's law of cause and effect creating jobs which in turn, creating wealth for those of us individually who will be hired to work and use the money we earn to acquire goods and services. Also, through the work that will be done, we are basically converting energy into action that will create something tangible or a certain beneficial act to those engaged to do the work and to the rest of us when we build bridges, highways, providing free healthcare, free education, and other needs.

So on one side of the ledger, we are unleashing forces that will enhance the quality of life of those who will gain employment. On the other side, we are simply making a bookkeeping entry estimating the value of the work performed, measured by a well-known and accepted units, namely, the dollars. The magnitude of that number on the spending side of the books will absolutely have no effect on our economics, whether it is in the thousands or in the trillions or higher.

In other words, when any of us is hired to work for all of us collectively, by the government, in any profession; an engineer, a carpenter, a doctor, or any other profession, that individual worker will be paid by spendable dollars that carry the full faith and credit of the U.S. Government, backed by all of us collectively.

To further clarify what we are saying and illustrate how nature works to provide all that we need, when we work, our bodies burn oxygen and consume food, to provide us with the needed energy so that we can convert it into action. That action can be manual, such as carpentry, plumbing, building, operating machinery, etc., or mental, such as teaching, writing, medical care, etc.

To replenish and accumulate energy, we have to eat and rest by sleeping. The plants (food) that we eat collect energy from the sun, using carbon dioxide and water (photosynthesis). So here we are; it is the sun that fuels the energy cycle for life. Surprisingly and astonishingly, under the prevailing economic system, we have been using a small part of it, measured in dollars, to give to the IRS as taxes to shape our future. Why? Is this not entirely unnecessary and without reason? And as we all know, the amounts of taxes that could be collected depends on how much taxable income is available, and that, of course, fluctuates at the mercy of the economic conditions at hand, including jobs and earnings that would be taxable.

So these are the facts upon which we can overhaul our economic system and do something that we can all celebrate for, and that is to say goodbye to the Internal Revenue and the tax collectors because they will no longer be needed and thus spare ourselves of all the agony and the hardships associated with the income-tax system. Those employees working for the IRS should be well provided for by making certain that they relocate to other assignments without interruption of pay.

So at this point, I need to say no more to convince ourselves that here is where our economic salvation lies, and we should take the plunge and overhaul our economic system as soon as possible. Economists and other opposing people cannot dispute the laws of nature and will have no legs to stand on. Let us be realistic; the magnitude of the increasing number on the debt side of the ledger for the amount of money being spent has no effect on anyone. It is simply a memo entry for reference purposes.

The time is here to light the way by introducing a bill in Congress to switch to the new economic system, and we the people should ask for it.

Taxes

First, let's go back in time to glance at the historic developments of taxes. Egypt ridiculously imposed a tax on cooking oil. Greece had to tax its people in order to finance the war, but it was later rescinded. Caesar Augustus initiated the inheritance tax to pay for the retirement of the military.

In England, taxes were first appeared during the Roman occupation. In the 11th century, according to a legend, Leofric, the Earl of Mercia, said he would reduce the high taxes which he had imposed on the residents of Coventry when his wife, Lady Godiva, agrees to ride naked through the town. The income-tax which we know today was actually designed by the British in 1800 to pay for the war with Napoleon. But in 1816, interestingly, opponents repealed it, citing that it should be used only to finance wars. The tax records were publicly burned by the Chancellor of the Exchequer. However, copies were retained in the basement of the tax court.

Here in America, most interestingly, in 1775, the time of the revolution, although Congress had no power to tax, nevertheless it printed paper money to pay for war expenses from 1775 to 1781, the value of which was backed by nothing. It was referred to as "immense heap of trash" continental dollars. The revolution had left much debt. Some money had to be borrowed from France. So to pay for it, excise taxes and tariffs were instituted, augmented by public land sale.

In 1789, Congress established the Treasury Department to oversee the land sale. It was in 1862, during the Civil War, that by necessity, President Lincoln and Congress created the position of Commissioner of Internal Revenue and started the income-tax to pay for the mounting war expenses. But ten years later, it was repealed. Once again, in 1894, Congress revived it, but again, in the following year, the Supreme Court shut it down as unconstitutional.

But in 1913, Wyoming ratified the 16th amendment, providing the three-quarter majority of the states needed to amend the Constitution, and that gave Congress the authority to institute income-tax.

At present, our monetary system is no longer backed by gold or silver. That was abandoned in 1971. So today we have flat currency, backed by the full faith and credit of the United States. However, based on the size and the strength of the U.S. economy, the U.S. dollar is the preeminent world-reserve currency. The print on the dollar bills reads,

"FEDERAL RESERVE NOTE. This note is legal tender for all debts public and private."

So history shows that wars were mostly instrumental in collecting taxes to pay for the mounting cost, and governments did at times abolish them later. Furthermore, people's inborn perception that newly issued money had to be backed by something valuable such as gold in order to be accepted. To this end, most likely, rather than creating new money, it appeared essential for governments to rely on existing money already earned by the people so that part of it would be collected through the income-tax system to meet the needs of the people. There are no compelling reasons to adopt such a flawed system.

But it is also evident that having a sizable and strong economy can create the essential confidence and reliability on its currency. Our superb credit worthiness diminishes the need for relying on the highly meager and insufficient income-tax to attend to our needs as a group, and it is time to discard it and remove the misery that has plagued humanity for a long time.

More of what we know about taxes: The *Merriam–Webster Dictionary* defines *tax* as "a compulsory contribution levied on . . . a heavy demand on one's powers or resources . . . An onerous duty or requirement." So why accept it and live under its atrocious rules and regulations if it is not necessary or justifiable?

Our current federal income-tax system, with its vastly complicated and excessive regulations and record-keeping requirements, which have evolved into monstrous proportions, enslaving us to adhere to its weird provisions and impeding the quality of life on our planet, not to forget its use as an instrument to manipulate the economy, should justifiably be put to rest and disappear without a trace. According to the CCH Standard Federal Tax Reporter, it would now take 74,608 8½ × 11 pages to contain the complexity of the code, stretching 187 times longer than it was a century ago.

Therefore, our existing federal income-tax code as well as inheritance tax should be totally wiped out from the face of the planet. We should gather all the tax regulations, place them on a rocket, and shoot it toward the sun, to be incinerated without a trace. Financial institutions will be spared the cost of maintaining records to report cost basis short- term and long- term holding periods when assets are sold—no more dividends and capital gains reports on forms 1099 and 1099B. Most happily, we humans will no longer have to file burdensome tax returns and maintain records for that purpose.

In light of the fact that education, healthcare, and infrastructure improvements will be funded by the federal government, states and local governments will not need many dollars to provide for police, fire, and other security protections. In addition, all outstanding state and municipal debts will also be paid by the federal government;

therefore, state incomes, sales, and inheritance taxes should be abolished by the states. However, appropriate low and reasonable real-estate levies (replacing the word *taxes*) may be imposed on owners commensurate with their choices of living. If one likes to live in a mansion with fifty rooms, it is justifiable to pay a real-estate toll higher than what his/her five-room-house neighbor pays. But income-taxes, if any, as well as sales taxes should, rightfully so, be abolished altogether by the states.

Let's not forget that although acting individually, we must have the money to accomplish what we desire. Now some of us who are lucky enough to own their homes can still expand their wealth by borrowing the money through mortgaging the real estate and easily have cash on the table. In this way, we can acquire other investments that could build up our wealth. This is why the rich can get richer and the poor stays poor. Mortgage and credit-card loans currently amount in the trillions. So clearly, the sooner we remove the IRS and the income-tax from our midst, the quicker we can vastly improve all aspects of living and hasten the day when we can achieve freedom from want.

Foreign entities who may wish to invest and maintain business in the United States may pay a surcharge on their gross sales. Such collections should be credited to a special income account, to be maintained for the purpose of augmenting our spending for research and development projects. Of course, such businesses will need dollars to pay for their employees. This need can easily be fulfilled by accumulating proceeds of sales. Banks may continue to lend money for mortgages and credit cards at the set fixed rates of 2% and 4% respectively.

Clearly, by justifiably abandoning the existing flawed economic system, we would unleash volcanic eruptions of prosperity across the land and hopefully the entire world.

To sum it all up, the picture is clear. Our current economic system is flawed. If we stay the course while the melting job market remains under the mercy of the blooming technology, the consequences will be disastrous. Most importantly, I repeat, there are no reasons that would compel us to stay with it and suffer. We can confidently acknowledge that the income-tax system has to be wiped out. Just knowing that the tax system would no longer exist would vastly enhance our peace of mind and confidence in our future. Just imagine—our elected officials will no longer have to quibble about having a budget in place, which is very difficult to agree upon.

And so now, having uncovered the roots of income-tax and what exactly it is, we can realistically define it as that part, as set by our representative government, of the total energy acquired from Mother Nature by a group of working people over a period of one year. Mother Nature does not want it back. It is time to say goodbye to Mr. Taxman.

Healthcare

Now that we have removed the income-tax system from our economics and lifted restrictions on vital spending, we can confidently establish a superb healthcare system, free for all regardless of the cost. In fact, by simplifying the system and taking advantage of allowing unrestricted use of the available technology such as MRI scans and other diagnostic tools, we will not only reduce costs in the long run but also find the causes of the illness sooner to speed up treatments and regain health wellness.

Just imagine—if we could have our genetic makeup examined soon after birth to identify those faulty genes and fix them, would that stamp out much of the sicknesses among us, shrink healthcare costs, and vastly improve the quality of life? Hopefully, under the new economic system, costs should no longer prevent us from taking full advantage of using the best tools available without hesitation. Let's be realistic. For any one of us, if a member of our immediate family falls ill and desperately needed help, would we not do all we can to restore good health regardless of costs when affordable?

The prevailing healthcare system, with all of its complicated procedures and crazy paperwork and reports, places unnecessary hardships on doctors and especially on seniors. In Medicare, we have to deal with atrocious requirements and rules: Part A, Part B, Medicap, HMOs, POS, copays, in network, out of network, referrals, prior approvals, deductibles, and more. The time spent every year during the enrollment period for the burdensome shopping around to find the most suitable plan places an unhealthy load on our life and creates stressful dynamics to make us sicker and increases anxiety, especially on the elderly, who need healthcare the most.

For example, just imagine if you are a senior with declining cognitive ability; you get a 200 page manual to swim through it to understand the mechanics of the healthcare program you have selected and the applicable cost to the treatment needed. How would you feel? So isn't it obvious by eliminating this crazy system, we will eliminate the inherent sicknesses caused by it?

Furthermore, the need to pay high out-of-pocket costs for undergoing vital tests to help determine the cause of our sickness, if one is fortunate to obtain approval from the insurance company, could deter some of us from taking such vital tests because it is not affordable. This could lead to increasing the health risk and the cost of the cure. One important part of healthcare that needs more care as we get older is dental care. There is little such protection under the Medicare system.

Good health is the crown achievement of life. We all know that living healthily promotes vitality, success, and endurance to pursue our goals. Most importantly, it lessens the dependence on other members of the family. Therefore, healthcare services must not be for profit and should be available freely with no red tape for all. Our system now is undisputedly miserable. It puts the healthcare insurance company's profits to reward the chief executive officer over our legitimate healthcare needs. Quite often some insurance companies would relegate medical decisions to an administrator sitting behind a desk to deny vital diagnostic and treatments services prescribed by our doctors to cut costs.

Understandably, insurance companies operate as profit-oriented entities owned by shareholders who invest their money to get rewarded through stock-price appreciation and dividends. By putting healthcare in their hands, we are creating a tug-of-war between two powerful opposing sides, one on the side of management's endeavors to beef up profits so it can increase the stock price, raise dividends to pay the investors, and justify pocketing high bonuses and generous returns through exercising stock options. One of the effective weapons in its arsenal is cutting costs and improving efficiency, but unfortunately, cutting costs is often spilled over to denying vital care. On the opposing losing side sits the fulfillment of our healthcare needs.

Let's not overlook where the dominant power in the drug industry resides. Clearly, for the sake of increasing profits, it has to firmly embrace the development and the marketing of new drugs, which eventually is sold as brand name or generic. This would naturally channel research investments in the direction of finding new drugs, often to treat the effects (symptoms) of the illness and increase sales rather than concentrating on the cause.

If more research is oriented towards fixing the genetic mechanism that could remove the disease altogether from our bodies, costs will go down, health restored, and the harmful and, at times, life-threatening side effects of the drugs would disappear. Providing healthcare not for profit, to be paid for collectively by the people, would certainly tip the scales in favor of extensive research to wipe out diseases altogether, to eliminate suffering, and substantially reduce healthcare costs.

Granted, there are some abuses in the system; a hospital once billed the insurance company $3,142.49 for a laboratory blood test. The insurance company paid $114.19 and adjusted (denied) $2,998.30, leaving a balance of $30.00 for the patient to pay. If we took the profit out of the equation, there will be no need for such financial gymnastics.

It is most distressing and hard to believe that some hospitals now require you to pay a parking fee to park in the Emergency Room parking area. Imagine you are having chest pain and want to rush to the Emergency Room for an immediate attention, and upon arrival, you discover that you need to know how to operate an electronic gate and have the means to pay for the parking fee before entry. Are we not risking a human life for the sake of the almighty dollar? In this case, it is not only the cost but also the method of collecting it.

Our healthcare system, with its copays and purposely hard-to-interpret its meaning and application, even by those who operate it, is totally screwed up and is a heavy burden on all of us, especially on seniors and doctors. Doctors' earnings are plummeting to the ground. This should not happen. How can we expect them to care for us without giving them what they deserve? I believe that by any measure, doctors and scientists should be placed on top of the pay-scale table. Nurses must also get what they deserve.

Operating health for profit and in so letting individuals sitting behind their desks and overruling doctors when a specific test such as an MRI and other treatments are needed just to cut costs and beef up the bottom line is detrimental to our well-being, motivating healthcare insurance companies' CEOs to find ways to unmercifully chisel all they can so they can get a higher bonus. The head is always responsible for any misconduct, even if such decisions are put in place by the underlings.

Shortchanging doctors and eroding their compensation will lead to the harmful shortage of physicians to the extent that well-suited and interested individuals will be discouraged from choosing this profession. Doctors have a unique responsibility to care and cure human illnesses.

A nonprofit free-for-all healthcare will have a vastly positive impact on society and on the business world. Employers will no longer shoulder the cost of healthcare, and employees will be spared the agony of finding coverage when leaving or switching employment and retiring. Employers' profits as well as workers' pay will go up. Moreover, much paperwork and waste will be eliminated.

Clinics in the manner of the Mayo Clinic should be spread out in cities and towns and made available within everyone's reach. People are gradually living longer and being more productive. Their lifetime-acquired knowledge in their fields of specialization can be beneficial to the rest of the people if they are encouraged to work longer. So we must create the appropriate healthcare maintenance to wipe out the infirmities of old age.

We stand at the dawn of highly promising breakthroughs in wiping out diseases through genetic manipulations. So money must not stand in the way of extensive research to reduce the costs of healthcare. Therefore, healthcare should be provided for all of us freely and without the unnecessary paperwork and the harmful delays in getting the needed treatment.

It is saddening to see most of us spending the final years of our life infirm, inundated with medication and suffering from the associated side effects. I believe that we can improve the quality of our final days of living by creating body-repair garages equipped with the up-to-date diagnostic and remedial instruments, allowing the infirm to check in for a complete and thorough overhaul. This dream can be fulfilled if we embrace the proposed economic system.

Education

The basic need for superior education is clearly having well-trained and highly knowledgeable teachers. Therefore, we must fulfill this requirement first to ensure the availability of knowledgeable, well-trained teachers at all costs.

In total, we all recognize that education is most vital for the well-being of each of us and all of us. It must be made available by us collectively to all ages for free and should not be managed for profit. Limiting college education to only those who can afford it can be detrimental to those who cannot. It is understandable that you will not need a degree to be a plumber or a carpenter and the like, but those who wish to embrace higher education should not be denied the opportunity for the lack of money.

The enlightenment of good education will benefit all of us if we have more rounded and knowledgeable humans. While we have established earlier that money should not stand in the way to do what we need to do collectively, students should not be saddled with the burden of paying the costs of their education. Furthermore, it is most important that we pinpoint the types of professions which require special training to fill open positions in the marketplace and train those who are suitable and willing to learn.

Sadly, the young among us have been faced with skyrocketing education costs. College costs have surged 500 % since 1985 with no end in sight. They are burdened with staggering student loans, with no assurance of getting a job upon graduation to enable themselves to make a decent living and to pay back their debt. What makes us superior to animals is that our brains can simulate the future and look ahead. When traveling, we think and plan in advance of what we need to prepare in order to reach our destination. We can and should plan ahead for our retirement. So it is not hard to predict what our destiny might be.

We are living at an age that tends us to use our bodies less and less as we move along. Making a phone call, we can simply press one button. To enter and leave a building, the doors open for us automatically. Cars that can drive themselves are now available for us. With technologies fast on the march, robotics shall engulf our surroundings and leave us with more idle time. As a result, we humans will have to take refuge in the arts, music, and science. Therefore, it would be rewarding for us to expose and familiarize our children with science and art at an early age.

Music appreciation is a good subject to teach as early as possible. The classics are the most important to know. It's shameful not to acquaint ourselves and appreciate the glorious music of the masters: Handel, Bach, Haydn, Mozart, Beethoven, Schubert, Schumann, Mendelssohn, Chopin, Liszt, and many others, as well as the American composers.

Learning how to draw and paint is a marvelous creative and satisfying hobby that endures with age. Science, particularly physics and biology, should be taught early in high school if not sooner. The universe is our home, so for us humans, learning about the basic laws of our universe are quite essential to our daily living. The more we know and understand its mechanisms and how we were created, the better for our happiness in understanding life.

Funds earmarked for education must include generous annual grants to libraries and the Arts. Individuals with rare talent, such as musicians who contribute to humanities well-being, should be sufficiently rewarded to foster their musical talents. The arts must also be nourished, providing opportunities for the advancements of the arts.

America's colleges remain the preeminent provider of education. They continue to be a magnet, attracting foreign students from all over the world. The more educated and enlightened people around the globe, the better for the rest of us. Therefore, making education free for all Americans should not shut the doors for foreign students. Certainly, it would be appropriate to require them to paying some tuitions and subjecting admission to space availability and keeping in mind that our students must come first.

Acquainting the students with the arts at an early age should be pursued vigorously. Such activities will come very handy in the future as leisure time will be plentiful.

Student Loans

On the day of transition to the new economic system, all outstanding student loans should be forgiven and recorded in subaccounts under the title of Forgiven Education Student Loans for historic reference purposes. There will be no need to pay back any outstanding student loans under the new economic system. This will be a great help in brightening the future of the students.

Disaster Recovery Funds

It is inconceivable to let fellow humans suffer the wrath of nature and lose their homes and belongings due to storms, hurricanes, earthquakes, tornadoes, meteors, and all other destructive catastrophes without immediate help. Provisions must be made to provide housing and lost necessities of living on an emergency basis, to be followed by the permanent restoration of housing and destroyed possessions. Money must not stand in the way to full restorations. To this end, it would be appropriate to maintain an inventory of empty homes throughout the land to provide immediate shelter where and when needed.

Rebuilding Infrastructure

Roads, highways, bridges, and all other infrastructure needs must be attended to and upgraded. This should provide work for the unemployed, thereby generating wealth while restoring health to our sagging infrastructure. We will be simply converting Mother Nature's ingredients into roads, bridges, and other construction's needs. Workers will not care whether or not we have cash available in the treasury account as long as they get credit for their contributions in the form of paychecks.

Under the existing economic system, you must have the money available to restore the dangerously degraded bridges. Loss of life as a result of collapsing bridges does not matter if we don't have the money to attend to proper maintenance and prevent the loss of life. At this time, most of the money needed to fix them before they fall comes from federal gasoline tax. That's understandable, but why it is not being done? The answer to that is not enough dollars are being generated from the gasoline tax, something that can be overcome by simply raising the gas tax. However, politically, raising the gas tax is not a good thing to embrace for getting elected. Now that we are abandoning the income-tax, there will be nothing to stop us to attend to what's needed, and we should proceed without delay.

Support For The Unemployed And Low Earners

Notwithstanding our efforts to provide work for the idles and train those who lose their jobs due to the impact of technology and other reasons to perform other suitable work, nevertheless, all those who are still unemployed, low earners, and the physically handicapped who need cost-of-living support should receive monthly assistance to meet their minimum needs. However, we must guard against any misuse of the system and make every effort to wipe out unemployment and idleness by testing those unemployed to determine the cause of their idleness and train them for a suitable work to the extent possible. We must diligently identify those who might be willingly to avoid work and live entirely on society's support and find work for them.

Research And Development

Unlocking the secrets of Mother Nature holds the key to our survival and attaining freedom from want. It is insane to curtail our research for the lack of money. The private sector has made worthy and valuable strides in investing in research and developments on all fronts. But regardless of its vital contributions, all types of research must be put on high gear. NASA must pursue unabated efforts to track down meteors and asteroids and develop effective methods to divert or destroy such intruders. Failure to do so, as I said earlier, humanity may follow the path of the dinosaurs and be wiped out in one blow.

The ongoing scientific discoveries have brought to light that our planet is virtually surrounded by a multitude of meteors and asteroids passing by our planet, and we have evidence of potential harm that a large chunk of rock penetrating the earth's atmosphere and hitting the earth can do most serious damage like incinerating a thickly populated city. Imagine a meteor hitting one of our electric nuclear reactors—perhaps another Chernobyl, Fukuyama, or where our nuclear bombs are stored. What can happen is most likely unimaginable damage.

Regrettably, we now do not have effective surveillance and tracking capabilities, and every now and then, we are told an undetected meteor or asteroid is about to closely pass us by. There can be no doubt that eventually, we will get hit, and we don't know when. We should not limit NASA's research to track these menaces due to the lack of funds. Moreover, we should develop capabilities to destroy or divert these space intruders away from our planet otherwise risk that danger of annihilation.

NASA has made efforts to track asteroids, but they haven't been as aggressive as the B612 scientists would like. B612 Sentinel is a nongovernmental voice whose mission is to discover and deflect asteroids away from the earth. In 1998, NASA established the Near-Earth Object Program office to detect potentially hazardous comets and asteroids. Recently, the agency announced a contest for scientists to develop asteroid-detecting algorithms, a year after a meteorite explosion in Russia had made international headlines. So we must restore NASA's funding to fulfill this most vital mission.

Lack of money has also shut the door on space explorations. Going back to the moon, traveling to Mars and beyond, and reaching for the stars should be vigorously pursued.

Harnessing nature's most powerful energy source, fusion, should give us unlimited source of energy with little waste. Just imagine—a bucket of water can generate power equivalent to millions of barrels of petroleum. What's wrong with nuclear energy is that when we split the uranium atom (fission), we create enormous amounts of nuclear waste that can remain active for perhaps millions of years. That can create a huge challenge in finding ways and places to store the waste. On the other hand, the longer we stay with fossil fuel, the more difficult it becomes to overcome any global warming.

If we reach the stage where the ice on the poles melts, the results would be catastrophic, causing huge displacements of people due to loss of shore lands. Fusion unleashes the nuclear energy of the sun by fusing hydrogen atoms, which is the energy source of the universe. If we can master fusion, we will have all the energy we need, leaving very little waste behind. Now you might say it's easily said than done, but we are created with mastering the ability to unlock the secrets of nature, and therefore, we should face the challenge.

Once the wall of money is dismantled, we will be freed to pursue research without hindrances or limits. Furthermore, genetic therapy has the potential of curing humanities ailments and maintaining a healthy society and substantially shrinking healthcare costs. Stem-cell research should be pursued vigorously. New printers that can spit out embryonic cell droplets that can grow to kidneys or hearts are within reach. The protection against the spread of dangerous diseases such as Ebola should not be denied funds that could curtail research.

And so we should keep in mind that in the creation process, we humans are endowed with intelligence allowing us to unlock the secrets of nature. We must expand our research efforts to exploit that knowledge as much as possible, not only to ensure our survival but also to constantly enhance the quality of life.

Retirement Social Security

It is imperative to set up a basic minimum support for the retirement of the elderly to meet their daily needs. Naturally, every individual is free to add his/her own savings from working and investments for retirement purposes, in addition to the money withheld from their wages for social-security retirement. People are living longer and need more income to live on comfortably if they don't wish to continue working. Now that we are taking the income-tax system away from the equation, Social Security funds should be kept separately and not comingled with other sources of savings or be used for other needs.

Moreover, it would be highly beneficial to invest one half of the saved social-security money in a sound portfolio of securities (stocks and bonds), to be managed by credible financial experts to enhance growth potential. The other half should be held in cash, earning interest and adjusted for inflation once a year. Withdrawals from these savings, pension, and all other retirement accounts, of course, will no longer be subject to paying tax under the new economic system as what we inappropriately do now. Without paying any tax will put more money in the pockets of seniors to enjoy life. We must also create the environment to encourage investments, to meet the demands of the growing senior population, who are now living longer, and to protect against inflation.

Insurance

We buy hazard insurance in order to minimize our losses and to recover the costs of repairing damages resulting from fires, floods, and the effects of natural forces. So the concept of pooling our contributions together in the form of premiums to meet the costs certainly makes good sense.

But having the insurance sold by entities operating for profit means that on top of the repair costs and aside from paying for the appropriate salaries of employees to do the administrative work, we also have to unnecessarily pay for dividends to the stockholders and higher premiums to beef up the companies' profits in order to increase the stock prices to attract people to invest in these companies as well as give managements bonuses and high returns through stock options when they beef up the bottom line.

Granted, to attract people to invest capital in these companies, it would be justifiable for them to expect healthy returns on their investments. But the crucial issue here is by doing so, we are creating inner dynamic forces to encourage paying the insured as less money as possible for the covered damages to increase the company's profits. So the question is, why should the insurance business be managed for profit? Why, why, why? There are no compelling reasons to do that whatsoever.

Therefore, it is clear that the right thing to do is for the government to establish nonprofit entities to administer insurance for all. Premiums should be set to meet the payout needs plus some cushion to be earmarked for implementing ways to reduce susceptibility and exposure to damages.

Therefore, life, flood, disability, hazard, and auto insurance need not be maintained on a for-profit basis. Such entities should be maintained under government supervision. Unquestionably, this would drastically reduce the costs of insurance because those who will be performing the administrative work will not have to pay dividends to the shareholders and will have no stock to raise its market price. With respect to life insurance, any excess in the amounts needed to pay for claims should be distributed to the insured as dividends, with the option of reinvesting the money in increasing coverage amounts or by lowering premiums.

To cite a good and well-documented example of an actual occurrence testifying to the serious misconducts of insurance companies, which would clearly provide a realistic comparison between the for-profit insurance with the not-for-profit insurance. As a Veteran, I had acquired a government-sponsored-and-operated life insurance policy for $10,000, effective February 28, 1984, paying a quarterly premium of $98. After being discharged from service, I continued paying premiums until now without interruption.

After joining the work force in the private sector, through my employer, I acquired a life-insurance policy from a supposedly highly reputable insurance company in the amount of $420,000 by paying a premium of $470.19 per month through payroll deductions, with the understanding that I can continue to maintain the policy if I switched jobs and after retirement.

Here comes the bullet which I could not dodge. Upon my retirement, the premium for continuing my policy stunningly soared from $470.19 to an entirely outrageous and unaffordable sum of $2,947.30; that is 6.268 times of what I have been paying. So I was compelled to walk away and drop the policy as the cost became prohibitive.

And so all those premiums which I had paid this damned insurance company were swallowed in its profit belly. I asked the insurance company, "Why the steep climb in the premium?" and was told, "that because you are no longer part of a group." So the cost for paying my premium singularly and directly to the company had to go up more than six times. I often wonder about how we humans exploit each other unmercifully in such ruthless and dishonest ways and who is to be blamed for such a shameful policy. I am reminded of an old saying: the fish always smells from the head. Hence, regardless of who in the company initiates such cruelty, the head must bear the blame.

To help others not to fall in this trap, I wrote a letter to the Director of Benefits of my former employer, reporting my anxiety and chastising the company for not requiring the insurance company to spell out upfront such rate increases when the participant is no longer in the group and to make it known to the employees before signing up for the plan. As you may guess, there was no response.

Now let's go to the other side to show the difference between for-profit and not-for-profit. The premiums collected from me under my VA life insurance policy, which I continued to pay without interruption, had created healthy surpluses in the earned premium pool. So over the years, I was given the option of either receiving dividends in cash or reinvesting the money in additional principal insurance to enhance the face value of my policy. I opted to reinvest. So thanks to Uncle Sam, as of February 24, 2017, my insurance policy, which had started with a face value of $10,000, had appreciated to $27,868 and is still growing. There you have it! Do I need to say more?

Utilities

The prevailing system of supplying water, heat, and electricity by companies operating for profit is not cost friendly to the average family simply because prices can suddenly jump up to high unaffordable rates, creating unbearable financial hardships despite holding hearings to make a case and justifying the increase. Therefore, it is vital that these necessities of living—water and electric and heating energy—be made available at cost and not for profit with a limit on the size of any one-time increase.

We must, as a society, carefully examine our resources and our present and future demands for energy to ensure that availability and consumption are within protected parameters. Research and development must play a significant role in developing energy sources to meet the growth in population.

As we cited before, Fusion, harnessing the energy of the stars, is in sight, and we must hasten the day to see it happen. It must be placed in the forefront of our eyesight and not let research and development be hampered by lack of money. Once the proposed new economic system is adopted and cost will no longer be an issue, our success can be met much sooner. Realistically, this vital necessity of living should be treated like healthcare and education and provided to all for free.

Food

If this new economic system is adopted, there will be no need for food stamps as most citizens will have jobs and should be self-sufficient to take care of their needs. However, we must see to it that food production meets the consumption level of the growing population. Moreover, as we acquire more robotic muscle, the cost of farming and producing food should decrease substantially. Agriculture could flourish without much labor to triple production.

We are now living at a time that holds promise of good things to come, unless, of course, we self-destruct. Technology is advancing at exponential rates. Science fiction is becoming a reality. With the 3D printer, we will be able to build lighter parts in the airlines industry to lighten the weight of airplanes and save fuel costs. NASA has much interest in this technology for making parts in space on demand.

The day may come when *Star Trek*'s amazing replication technology, which works at the molecular level to synthesize materials to instantly produce any object, including food, may not be far away. Just imagine the impact such a technology will have on our life. Poverty and Hunger will be no more. Is it not self-defeating to allow money to hold us back from expediting the achievement of this priceless technology? In any event, until then, we must not let anyone endure hunger.

Transportation

We drastically need to upgrade our transportation system. Our highways require much upgrading, especially now that self-driving cars are increasingly showing up on the roads. Faster rail travel is doable, and we should switch to the much faster lev-trains concept. Other countries have already done that. The safety of flying has to be enhanced with a much more improved air-traffic control system. We should invest as much as needed in modernizing our airports and upgrading our transportation system, with emphasis on safety.

Defense

"Speak softly and carry a big stick" was the centerpiece of foreign policy of President Theodore Roosevelt. He described his style of foreign policy as "the exercise of intelligent forethought and of decisive action sufficiently far in advance of any likely crisis." Negotiating peacefully with our enemies to avoid the use of force stands to score a higher degree of success when having and brandishing that big stick. Maintaining a big stick is unquestionably an effective deterrent and can spare us the huge cost of wars and the loss of precious life.

Obviously, two world wars and other conflicts have not bestowed any wisdom on the human race to settle differences peacefully. Regrettably, the levels of maturity and perception do not advance equally among us in the evolution process, leaving some behind under the banner of the caveman's protective aggressive behavior.

National, ethnic, and religious divisiveness still generate hatred and carry serious threats to our freedom and safety while we wish to preserve our way of life. The emergence of employing self-sacrificed human bombs by some of the human race to fight, and to vent their hate, and to force their ideology on us adds much seriousness to the task to identify infiltrated enemies, requiring strong intelligence and heavily guarded borders with stricter immigration laws to keep away unwanted immigrants and visitors. Therefore, budget cuts in defense spending would be a serious mistake. We need to maintain a strong and technically and scientifically advanced fighting force empowered with daring and cunning intelligence. We must give our veterans the respect and the credit they deserve. Amputees deserve lifetime support and need not be supported shamefully by charitable contributions.

International Debt

The existing foreign and all other debts will remain secure as always and can be paid as usual upon maturities without renewals. Furthermore, holders of the debt should be given the option of cashing in and receiving cash for the lent amount plus accrued interest at any time of their choosing.

The economic strength, productivity, and talent of our people offer unmatchable strength to our credit worthiness. Our dollar will continue to retain its worthiness to buy goods and services throughout the world as usual. Under the new economic system, there will be no need for our government to borrow money. However, treasury instruments may continue to be issued, allowing foreign entities, governments, and U.S. citizens to buy them but at a low rate of interest simply to provide a safe haven for investors to maintain liquidity.

Charity

Charitable contributions have been an instrument for reducing taxes by the wealthy while filling some of the vacuum in many sectors of living. Besides, the questionable authenticity of some charitable collections and the costs associated with administering them can render them unworthy. Moreover, they can never solve or cure the illnesses that exist among us, stemming from the lack of availability of money. With the current tax code out the window and the unlimited availability of funds for research and development, charitable contributions will not be needed but may continue if people feel getting inner satisfaction and pleasure by helping others. It is part of our inner nature to make charitable contribution to help others.

The Steering Seven

The task of this group is to keep us one step ahead of the future and be ready for what follows—indeed the most challenging undertakings. This group should be selected by the President from a pool of the most brilliant minds our country can offer without regard to color or gender. They must be scientifically oriented and selected from each field of endeavor: physics, biology, finance, defense, and security protection, and all other essentials of living.

Their mission should be heavily concentrated on ensuring the balancing of food availability with population growth, the fulfillment of energy needs to the growing population, the safest method of facilitating places to live in, including whether to live in crowded cities or spreading out to more open land (high-rise versus low-level quarters), and the construction of houses with fireproof material. Most importantly, we should do all that is possible to ensure that we constantly strengthen our capability to destroy and deflect asteroids and meteors away from our planet, placing heavy emphasis on research and development on harnessing the power of the sun (fusion).

It is quite obvious, as we discussed earlier, that the advancements in technology and the proliferation of robotics will eliminate jobs in many sectors of the working force on an ongoing basis. Therefore, we urgently need to ready ourselves to deal with these inevitable occurrences and plan in advance to find jobs for those workers who will most likely lose their jobs and train them in other appropriate work ahead of time.

Furthermore, there is no doubt that citizens will have more idle time in the future, that could encourage unwanted behavior and mischief. Training people to acquire worthwhile hobbies at an early age, such as the arts, music, writing memoirs, reading history and science, and other beneficial practices, should make life more enjoyable for all and foster more friendly conduct among the people.

Implementation

Undoubtedly, we need to devise an orderly transitional approach, one that leaves clear imprints of our footsteps to the new economic system.

It seems logical that the first step that should be taken before we do anything is for congress to pass a bill with the approval of the president, setting forth the minimum percentage (e.g., 70%, 80%, 90% or more) of the voting public, that should be required to approve the transition to the new economic system before the new system is presented to the public for a vote.

Furthermore, in the event the bill is not passed by the public by the required majority after the first vote, how many times may we be able to vote again? Although it would be highly unlikely for the bill not to pass on the first attempt, nevertheless three times would be a reasonable number. If it is approved by the required majority of the citizens, then we can proceed with the implementation process. In view of the fact that the new economic system will be highly beneficial to all of us, rich and especially poor, there will be no opposition.

We should set in place a simple accounting methods whereby separate accounts are maintained for each spending category, such as healthcare, education, defense, energy, science, food, shelter, government, municipal operations, and any other vital recognizable necessitates to keep track of spending in each category. In addition, the following accounts should be opened on the books.

Master Expense Account to which all the above mentioned expense account balances should be transferred at the end of the fiscal year. This will provide a clear historical picture of our spending in each category from year to year and the accumulation of our ongoing credit grants (money) earned for work done. We can appropriately name this account as The Economics Freedom Account.

Transitional expense account should be opened to take over the current treasury debt, which can be paid immediately, for eventual transfer of the balance to the Master Expense Account. Also, another transitional account for the income being collected from the flowing taxes, up to the date of conversion or beyond, to receive stragglers' payments. This credit balance can simply be transferred to the Transitional expense account.

The changeover day should be celebrated annually as a holiday for all times to come to remind us of our old flawed economic system. We can name it Economics Freedom Day.

It is most likely that all nations would eventually follow our footsteps and adopt our new economic system once we get started. It would be advantageous to all humanity to follow our footsteps and adopt similar economic systems. The International Monetary System should be engaged to lend a hand in technical assistance to those countries that will need assistance to make the transition. We should do all we can to help because there are many countries still lagging behind economically.

Implementing the new plan may not be so easy in the beginning, but we should keep it simple. Let's not forget that with our concentrated collective action, we will drastically change and enhance the quality of our life and create a much healthier and well-educated society. It would be imperative to maintain a semblance of order and accountability with utmost simplicity. Mortgage rates should be set at 2% and credit card interests at 4%. In this way, everyone will be treated equally.

The Private Sector

In light of the fact that the creation of business entities to produce marketable goods and services would undoubtedly come from the intellectually inventive capability of those who conceive the product and from investors who are willing to provide capital for implementing the business and, furthermore, since there is no income-taxes to pay and share the profit with the government, it is fitting that the profits earned from the business should go to the owners and to the investors.

Although the employees are being paid for their work, under such a profit-oriented working climate, they should also be rewarded by receiving a share of the profits in cash or in stock, ideally both. And management should see to it that such a policy is put in place. It would be reasonable that this will be done voluntarily by management to stay competitive in the marketplace as the demands for workers will be constantly on the rise.

However, the power of incentive must remain dominant nationwide and especially in the private sector. The advancement in all sectors of life on our planet, from medical to technological, is the inventions of individuals. The simplification of our economic system and the removal of the cost-of- the health-care burden from the shoulders of employers should encourage entrepreneurial spirit to reduce sales prices and increase employees' pay. This should boost the workers' earnings and their share in the success of the business.

We should maintain the simplest system and keep inflation at bay. Punishing companies with large fines by the government for the management's misdeeds as we do now can only hurt owners and the shareholders and harms the company's future. Any needed punishments should be placed on the shoulders of those who committed the misdeeds and removing them from their positions. This would be a better approach. Furthermore, it would be fair that companies should compensate those who sustained financial losses due to the damaging misconduct of management.

Wall Street

Unquestionably, Wall Street is a key player in the economy of our country and the world at large. Despite the hatred that people feel about what it does, it is the place where the seeds for wealth creation are planted. When a business venture has the smell of success, it must have capital to build its business and to increase its production, leading to higher sales, thus creating the need to hiring more workers and creating jobs. The more of us have jobs, the more money we can earn to spend and put more life in the economy.

Enabling companies to acquire cash to expand their business, Wall Street will facilitate that by working with business entities to design a suitable approach. If the companies happen to be private, it will open the path to make them public companies, owned by stockholders, and make public offerings to sell the stock to interested buyers and thus raise the cash needed to expand and acquire the capability for future expansion. The partners of the private companies could greatly benefit and cash in by selling some of the shares they now own.

Companies which are already public could still raise cash to expand their business by issuing more shares of common stock as well as shares of preferred stock and bonds if deemed advantageous. So this is the source through which wealth is created.

Wall Street is also the home of the New York Stock Exchange (NYSE), where trading is carried out. Indeed, it is the trading hub for ours and the world's economy, and thus, it has an enduring impact on the global economy.

With the elimination of the feeble income-tax system, Wall Street firms will be able to breathe comfortably. The tremendous hardships of the existing regulations, record keeping, and reporting will vanish. Operating costs should plummet to a low unimaginable level—no more forms 1099s to report interests and dividend income earnings, likewise no more 1099Bs to report long-term or short-term income or loss amounts, as well as acquisition and sales dates, cost basis, and sales proceeds. Such records become the shareowner's choice to maintain should he or she wants to keep track of the progress of the investments.

However, we should learn from the past and ban Wall Street from selling derivatives and any similar products, which could be hard for the public to understand their make ups. Also, there is always the product of greed, that prompts some of us to defraud others. Heavy penalties should be imposed on those responsible. But we can safely predict that under the proposed economic system, where there is no more income-tax and the gates of prosperity are wide open, improved conduct should be expected to prevail.

The Fed

The Federal Reserve Bank was created by Congress during President Woodrow Wilson's term in office on December 23, 1913. To foster the Fed's mandate is "to promote sustainable growth, high levels of employment, and stability of prices to help preserve the purchasing power of the dollar and moderate long-term interest rates." In my personal opinion as a layman observer, despite the sharp criticism of Chairman Ben Bernanke, I think he has done a remarkable job in keeping the ship afloat and in saving the country from diving into deeper recession. Janet Yellen also deserves the same credit by not rushing to raise interest rates.

In other words, the Fed's job is to foster a sound banking system and a healthy economy. To accomplish its mission, the Fed serves as the banker's bank, the government's bank, the regulator of financial institutions, and the nation's money manager.

The U.S. Treasury has a checking account with the Federal Reserve. All revenues generated by taxes and all outgoing government payments are handled through that account. Included in this service, the Fed sells and redeems government securities such as savings bonds, treasury bills, notes, and bonds. In short, the Federal Reserve Board acts as the policeman for banking activities within the United States and abroad.

The Fed also issues all coin and paper currency. The U.S. Treasury actually produces the cash, but the Fed Banks would distribute it to financial institutions. It's also the Fed's responsibility to check bills for wear and tear and to take damaged currency out of circulation. The Fed also sets margin requirements for investors to buy stocks and bonds by borrowing the money.

The Fed should continue its assigned duties, but of course, the management tasks will be somewhat different because our spending outlays will no longer be dependent on income-tax receipts and money supply. But its task for issuing the required credits to attend to our needs will be much harder because of the responsibility to validate the legitimacy of the requested credit. In this respect, we should put in place appropriate procedures for authorizing payments for implementing the job at hand and guard against abuse.

Furthermore, it seems fair, as we said before, to set the mortgage interest rates at a low rate of 2% to promote home ownership. It is essential to foster a feeling of comfort and security to help every family to own a home. It would also be more accommodating to those who might be in need to borrow money; the Fed would preferably be empowered to set up a credit-card low interest rate in the tune of 4%.

It would be imperative for the Fed to monitor and harness inflation and create effective restrictions to keep it at bay. The absence of income-tax coupled with human greed can create inner dynamics for increasing profits. While the economy is operating at high gear, full employment should prevail. This would naturally lead to putting more cash in the pockets of the people and increase demands for goods and services. That, of course, can drive prices higher. The right thing to do is for companies to increase production of the sought-out goods to increase sales, thereby increasing profits instead of increasing prices. It would be fitting for the Fed, if necessary, to limit and control price increases to keep inflation at bay.

Other responsibilities of the fed; such as setting up banks' reserve requirements and setting the discount rate, which is the interest rate that banks pay on short-term loans from a Federal Reserve Bank and Open-Market Operations (the Fed constantly buys and sells U.S. government securities in the financial markets, which, in turn, influences the level of reserves in the Banking system) all these should remain in the hands of the Fed. Remember, the end goals of monetary policy are sustainable economic growth, full employment, and stable prices.

Immigration

We all know America is a nation of immigrants with a big heart who will help the people of other nations in times of need, particularly when natural disasters strike, but we must act within our means and live up to the principle that charity begins at home. Our country and its citizens must come first. We should help other people as much as possible as long as we are not dragged down by the process. The gates of illegal immigration must be shut tightly.

Some of us may like to see living with open borders, but this would be highly risky at the present time because, as stated earlier, people's standing in the evolution process are not equal. Some of us are still clinging to the Dark Ages mentality and can be inspired to become terrorists or can become criminals.

If this proposed economic system is put in place, providing citizens with free healthcare and education and all other protective elements of living without paying income-taxes, you can bet your last dollar on the side that the entire inhabitants of the planet would want to be here with us. Therefore, although we are a nation of immigrants, nevertheless it would be imperative that our immigration laws be instituted under a strict formula, taking into account how many immigrants we can absorb within a set time period. The health, and the economic capabilities, of the immigrants and the ability to contribute to society must also be taken into account. Certainly, there are those who have special talents and capabilities who may be needed to fill in vacant jobs in our country. Nevertheless, they must still be checked out and enter the country legally.

Most importantly, it would be fair and reasonable to make certain that those who wish to come and live with us must abide by the laws of the land and are able to speak the American language. Otherwise, they must learn it before applying for immigration. Furthermore, in light of the emergence of terrorism worldwide, immigrants should be in-depth vetted regardless of where they come from. Naturally, those found having ties with terrorist organizations should not be allowed to enter the country. No doubt, living under tight security is most vital to our well-being. In this regard, our Commander in Chief must be left free to use all tools available to ensure the protection of all citizens, including the incoming new immigrants.

If our new economic system is implemented, we will be envied by the rest of the world. Through technology and the Internet and the flood of information from all parts of the world, the nations' boundary lines are becoming much paler. Let's not forget that despite the fact that we are not genetically created equal because evolution does not advance uniformly, it would still be most beneficial for all of the inhabitants of our small planet to lend a hand to those who lag behind and do what we can to lift them up. To the extent of how much interference other governments would allow us to participate in designing a suitable economic system for their countries, we should offer our help to create appropriate ways to improve the life of the inhabitants of other nations. If we don't do that, we will face the danger of serious intrusions by outside forces.

Foreign Aid

America is a blessed land and generous. Historically, when natural calamities strike any part of the planet, we spare no effort to lend a hand. To nations that depended on us over the years to provide financial support, to stay strong, and maintain their standings among other nations, it would be ill-advised to deny them our support. However, our support should be provided commensurate with their needs and the availability of our resources.

Export And Import

It would not be hard to predict the effects of the new economic system on exporting goods to foreign countries and importing them. However, we can expect that under the new economic system, most likely, full employment and higher wages will be dominant across the land. But with paying no income-taxes, employers will be restrained from moving their business outside the country.

However, if the cost of foreign labor is substantially below domestic costs, the quality of the manufactured goods, foreign versus domestic, should play a part in choosing which goods to buy. Nevertheless, if the cost of manufacturing goods abroad and selling them in the U.S. market is very profitable, we should consider imposing high tariffs on importing such goods.

But let's not forget that despite the prosperity—full employment, high wages, and declining availability of workers—there still will be wind flowing from the opposite direction, influenced by the ongoing and emergence of new technologies that could enhance the availability of idle workers in our labor market.

There are still the need for raw materials, which may be plentiful in other parts of the world, to produce the goods. Naturally, this will have to be negotiated as to the price, choice of currency, and exchange rate. Although it might become difficult to set the currency-exchange rate, but most likely, when our new economic system is implemented, the markets will automatically reflect the resultant adjusted rates.

On the export side, the prices for the goods to be purchased from us, of course, while being negotiated, should also determine which currency will be used, the seller's or the buyer's, as well as the exchange rate.

The Supreme Court

When the U.S. Constitution was written on September 17, 1787, by James Madison, with considerable contributions by Thomas Jefferson, Thomas Paine, and John Adams—George Washington is credited with the responsibility of overseeing the Constitutional Convention that took place in Philadelphia between May 5, 1787, and September 17, 1787—it was left in the hands of Congress to decide the number of justices required to serve on the Court. In 1789, Congress set the number to five Justices and one Chief Justice. But over the years, Congress has passed various acts to change this number from a low of five to a high of ten. In 1869, the number was set at nine and has not changed since.

It might be interesting to know that in 1789, the chief Justice's salary was only $4,000 and the Associate Justice $3,500. For now, the Chief Justice earns $255,500 and the Associate $244,500. Only one President, William H. Taft, had also served as a Supreme Court Justice.

Surprisingly, however, there was no term limits imposed that would say how long Supreme Court Justices could serve. But it was stated that Justices "shall hold their offices during good behavior." So accordingly, they can stay at work for as long as they wish unless impeached by the House of Representatives and convicted by the Senate. Historically, only one Associate Justice, Samuel Chase, in 1805, was impeached by the House, but the Senate acquitted him.

Considering the fact that humans are now living longer than when the Constitution was written and that the Supreme Court plays a crucial part in the affairs of our country, particularly in interpreting the U.S. Constitution, and has the final word in deciding the outcome of cases which had been tossed around in lower courts, it now appears justifiable that we reexamine the wisdom of not setting up a retirement age for the Justices or making certain that their health status is in good shape to meet the demands of that office. It is a matter of fact that their personal health struggles can influence their decisions, and we must guard against such possibilities.

Choosing Our Leaders

To ensure that we elect the best available leaders, particularly the President, to protect our way of life, keep our country safe, and guide us to a promising future, we must employ the best sources available to us and create effective means towards that end. At present, our leaders come from all walks of life with and without having any related qualifications to fill that position. Money and party affiliation play major roles to get elected.

I ask this question; if we have top-notch academies to give us our military leaders, why not require our educational entities to make available special training courses with the help and the input of former presidents for those of us who may decide to run for high offices?

Also, setting up specific criteria for the office of the president, in addition to being a natural-born citizen (a citizen from birth) and having attained the age of thirty-five, it would also be helpful for the candidate to be well grounded in political science, the military, and physics to be familiar with and understand the basic laws of nature.

It might even be desirable to undergo a boot-camp-style military training for a preset time period. Such training will give us well-rounded individuals to do the job of the Commander-in-Chief and protect our country from any harmful foreign aggression. However, such qualifications should not be written in stone because highly gifted and innately wise individuals with well-rounded experience who may not be seeking election to the office of the president may emerge unexpectedly under the force of nature. Such rare individuals should be persuaded to serve.

We must reconsider allowing political contributions to be an expression of freedom of speech and whether or not to leave the door open for citizens to using money to influence our thinking and voting decisions by those who have money that may do this for their own benefit. To promote the true democratic process, candidates should get equal funding and time to make that convincing presentations about their fitness to be elected. Furthermore, the health conditions and the ages of those who seek the offices of the president and the vice president must be taken into consideration to qualify them to run for those offices. Such candidates should be required to undergo thorough physical and mental exams before throwing their hats in the ring.

At any rate, we are living in an age where it is within our grasp to eliminate human suffering, whether it is economics or medical in nature. We have the tools and the know-how to do it. We should not hesitate to use all the resources we have to achieve what we want. It is very critical, therefore, that we elect the best qualified individuals who can achieve our sought-out goals. We must guard against allowing gender or color to influence our choice.

Overcoming Side Effects

We have to be smart and seriously consider how to deal with the power of the side effects that could result by achieving our sought- out objectives in all sectors of living. For example, if we succeeded in curing cancer, on one side, it will prevent the devastating suffering that humanity has to bear since walking on the planet. The cost savings that can be achieved will be huge. But, it is most important that we also look at the other side of the coin. Can you imagine how many healthcare workers currently engaged in cancer-related services will be out of work?

We can clearly see here that at present, there are inner powerful dynamics against succeeding to achieve our goal, embedded in the system. Therefore, to overcome this obstacle, we should make it known up front that we have a plan in place that will deal with this issue and restore job losses and see to it that those affected regain their security and comfort of living if success is achieved to cure cancer. This should remove the tendency to discourage and slow down the progress aimed at achieving the goal of curing this devastating disease.

Undoubtedly, such an obstacle would exist in other sought-out objectives. To name a few, in the medical field alone, we want to cure diabetes, heart disease, asthma, nervous disorders, and other ailments that are creating much suffering to humanity. In the field of dentistry, scientists believe that we may see a day when our bodies can regrow lost teeth. Such a wonderful achievement will be a major step towards healthy living and will vastly enhance the joy of eating. It will render all those dental remedies which we all dislike obsolete. But that will also create a huge financial loss to dentists and those engaged in servicing it. Here, again, we must be considerate and provide the means to restore the resultant financial losses to this group.

In other fields, such as the energy-producing facilities, job losses can be very substantial if we succeeded in harnessing the energy of the sun through fusion, which, by the way, many scientists believe it is coming. Here also, the extent of savings will be enormous. But many workers who are engaged in the field of oil production will lose their jobs and the income they need to sustain their comfort of living. Therefore, we must make it known to these workers that they will be protected.

In taking a giant step to overhaul our current flawed economic system, it should be expected that some side effects can emerge that will require immediate resolution. This will be the job of the Steering Seven to come up with the needed remedy.

Another area that should be watched is the ugly inflation. High incomes could easily increase demands on goods and services, which could easily light the fire of inflation. As stated earlier, the Federal Reserve Bank will be keeping a watchful eye to control it. Luckily, however, in one important sector of the economy, with the likelihood of increasing the use of robotics in agriculture, the increase in food prices will be highly unlikely; nevertheless, we should not let it happen.

There is still another area that we should keep under watch. With guaranteed living in comfort, with free healthcare, and free education, some of us might attempt to evade work and not contribute to society. Hence, we must determine the reason for such a stance and find work for them and train them for suitable jobs, unless they are handicapped or legitimately retired. With the floodgates of prosperity are wide open, it should not be difficult to find jobs for them.

In taking such a giant step to overhaul our flawed economic system, it should be expected that some issues will rise to the surface that will require some adjustments. Again, the Steering Seven should be able to provide corrective steps that need to be taken.

Conclusion

In conclusion, after weighing the advantages and the disadvantages of this new unparalleled and futuristic economic system, which could be considered ahead of its time, you could say that we humans are not there yet and do not deserve it. Nevertheless, the benefits will be undeniably and vastly outweighing any disadvantages that may come to the surface. Look at it this way; when living under unprecedented security to protect our liberty and with no worries about not having roofs over our heads and of not having the ability to feed our children, we are laying powerful dynamics for living with peace of mind and happiness.

Furthermore, when money is not standing in the way of research and development, we can readily accelerate our activities in this field to unlock the secrets of Mother Nature. This is where the promising future of humanity lies. Scientists believe that astounding discoveries are within our reach.

Just imagine— if we continue to harness nature's powers, perhaps even attaining the ability to control the weather, human conduct will change for the better. The aggression stance in us should abate, crime should diminish, and jails should empty out when people will take their eyes off the dollar sign.

In any event, although the chances of adopting this revolutionary, realistic, and sorely needed economics changeover, at this stage of our lives it may not be as favorable as it should be—, and perhaps we are not ready for it yet—in the least, we are planting the seeds for its eventual adoption. But we should not wait. The sooner we discard the current economic system, the better.

It's very likely that those who choose to oppose the proposed economics overhaul would argue that we might be placing a very heavy load on the shoulders of the government to manage all vital services that shape our lives, including healthcare, education, social security, and other protective services, and may shy away from leaving such services in the hands of the government. But we have clearly demonstrated that these vital services must not be operated for profit. In fact, there is no apparent reason for the government not to adopt special incentives to attract highly capable and talented people out of the pool of the most qualified individuals that could carry out the work as done in the hands of the private sector.

Going a step further, qualified entities within the private sector could be engaged by the government to administer such services as an extension of the government on a not-for-profit basis by creating a competitive environment. Just look at the defense industry, which is now operated by the private sector for all of us. Although for profit, is it not the best in the world? It certainly is.

Other opponents may say that most of the human race is not mature enough and indeed not ready or deserving to embrace such a phenomenal mode of living without the day-to-day struggles and without abusing it. Furthermore, if well fed and provided for, including free healthcare and education, some will create mischief and trouble for the rest of us and may demand more.

This may be possible, but if we weigh the good and the bad, we simply cannot ignore the stark reality that staying on our present course will put us on the path of suffering from overwhelming economic hardships. But without any doubt, we must guard against outside intrusion because living under such comfort and security, the whole world would want to be part of it. Of course, it would be in our best interest to help other countries ride the waves to prosperity if they let us.

Furthermore, we should guard against the possibility that some of us, while living under the tent of economic security, might become self-indulgent and degenerate people. To help avoid such a problem, we should encourage people to get acquainted with the arts from an early age in school. This is an important challenge for the Steering Seven to deal with.

Let's not forget that with the quest of unabated research and developments to unlock the secrets of nature, we might see the face of what is now considered science fiction to become a reality. It is not out of the realm of possibility that we could succeed in building replicators to create what we need, thereby eliminating scarcity altogether and giving us more spare time to enjoy life.

A tricorder that could easily diagnose illnesses, as demonstrated by *Star Trek*, is now in the process of being built. Hence, the proposed economic system would serve as a bridge to a new mode of healthy and enjoyable living, allowing us to pursue the fulfillment of our dreams and let science, art, music, and poetry flourish across the land. So with more idle time at hand, we must guard against self-indulgence and becoming degenerate people.

So at this point, I feel confident that I have made the case and lifted the veil to show that our economic system is flawed and unjustifiable and that there are no compelling reasons for us to live with it and suffer its slings and arrows and that it should be abandoned. The human brain is a marvelous instrument indeed, and it makes me wonder and ask, could it be that as part of our creation process, our brains can intuitively capture ideas floating through space-time to fulfill our destiny as inscribed in the book of evolution?

Just compare how life was when the caveman walked on the land with how we live today. It appears plausible that barring insanely incinerating ourselves in a nuclear inferno, this proposed economic change might simply be a step towards the fulfillment of that destiny. By diligently concentrating on research and development to unlock the mechanics of nature, we can have whatever we desire, and freedom from want can be within our grasp.

Art and music contribute to our well-being and prepare us to fill and enjoy any leisure time that might come our way in the future. I have already embraced the arts to fill any spare time that may come my way and found that it greatly contributes to my well-being and enhances my appreciation and enjoyment of nature's beauty. I'm happy to show you these samples of my artwork in addition to the inspiring deer painting: three oil paintings of the lighthouses on Martha's Vineyard.

In closing, to summarize the basic mechanics of the proposed economic system, as humans, we will simply follow nature's design by harnessing the energy of the sun, by eating and sleeping to replenish our energy, converting food and water into action to work, and getting paid to take care of our personal needs. As stated before, we will be paid in dollars issued by our representative government as authorized by us the people. Such money will be issued, as done now, as a flat currency, backed by the full faith and credit of the United States without limitation and the need to pay back.

Most happily, we are locking the doors of the Internal Revenue Service and letting the unnecessarily burdensome income-tax system be gone with the wind, thus creating a healthy, secure, and enjoyable environment for all. Indeed, we will have the ability at hand to create heaven on earth. The question is, will we humans have the courage to meet that challenge now?

EDGARTOWN MARTHA'S VINEYARD LIGHTHOUSE

EDGARTOWN MARTHA'S VINEYARD LIGHTHOUSE

THE GAYHEAD LIGHTHOUSE ON
MARTHA'S VINEYARD

Index

A

account
  master expense, 91
  transitional expense, 91
accounts, retirement, 73
action, collective, 92
assets, 7, 12, 37, 50
  real-estate, 7
  tangible, 35

B

banks, 7, 52, 98–99
Bernanke, Ben, 97
bonds, 35, 73, 96, 98
business, 18, 51, 93–96, 104
  real-estate, 7
business entities, 14–15, 93, 95

C

capital, 75, 93, 95
capital gains, 50
Congress, 46, 48, 90, 97, 106
contributions, charitable, 85, 87
credit card, 52, 92
credit grants, 91

D

debt, 4–5, 13, 18, 31, 48–49, 61, 86
  national, 5
  treasury, 91

E

Economics Freedom Account, 91
Economics Freedom Day, 91
economic system, x–xiii, 3, 5, 7, 9–11, 13, 19, 27, 42–43, 45–46, 52, 91–92, 94, 112–13, 115–16
  existing, xi, 4, 6, 9, 26, 66
  flawed, 91, 112–13
  new, xi, 46, 53, 64, 74, 80–81, 85, 90, 92, 101, 104–5
  proposed, 59, 96, 100, 118–19
economy, healthy, 97
education, 4, 11–12, 23, 27, 40–44, 50, 60–62, 80, 91, 100, 113, 116–17
  free, 11, 27, 44, 113
  higher, xi–xii, 60
employment, 45, 97, 99, 104
energy, 6, 21–22, 24, 29, 38–39, 45, 71, 79, 88, 91, 112, 119
  nuclear, 71
experts, financial, 73

F

Federal Reserve Bank, 97, 99, 113
financial institutions, 50, 97–98
fiscal year, 91
Forgiven Education Student Loans, 64

G

goods, x, 6, 31–32, 34, 40, 44, 86, 99, 104–5, 113
  exchanging, 5, 31, 33
growth
  economic, 99
  sustainable, 97

H

healthcare, xi–xii, 4, 11–12, 14–15, 27, 29, 40–44, 50, 53–59, 71, 80, 91, 100, 111, 116–17
  free, 11, 27, 41–42, 100, 113, 117

I

immigrants, 85, 101
income-taxes, 4, 42, 47–48, 51–52, 67, 93, 96, 99, 104
income-tax system, 46, 49, 52–53, 73, 120
inflation, 11, 31, 34–35, 37–38, 40, 73–74, 94, 99, 113
insurance, 75–76, 78
insurance companies, 54–56, 76–78
interest rate, 6, 97, 99
  mortgage, 98
Internal Revenue Service (IRS), 45–46, 51, 120
investments, 31, 37, 51, 73–75, 96

L

loans
  credit-card, 51
  mortgage, 7
  short-term, 99
  student, 61, 64
losses, financial, 94, 112

M

market value, 7
monetary system, international, 92
Mortgage, 7, 37, 51–52

P

pension, 15, 73
private sector, 15, 24, 69, 77, 93, 116–17
profits, 24, 37, 55–58, 60, 75–76, 79, 93, 116–17
  increasing, 55, 99

R

rates, mortgage, 92
recessions, ix, 5, 7, 11, 97
research and development, xi, 13, 18, 43, 69, 79, 87–88, 115, 118–19
retirement, 47, 61, 73, 77

S

savings, 7, 36–37, 40, 73, 97–98, 112
  government, 5
services, x, 5–6, 17, 31, 33–34, 40, 44, 55, 77, 86, 93, 98–99, 113, 116–17
  vital, 17–18, 116
shares, 11, 37, 93–96
society, x–xi, 5, 10–11, 22, 27, 29, 31, 33, 41, 43, 58, 79, 101, 113
solution, realistic, 10

sound banking system, 97
space explorations, 18, 70
stocks, 35, 37, 55, 73, 75–76, 93, 95–96, 98

T

taxes, 7, 46–51, 74, 97
  gas, 67
  inheritance, 47, 50–51
technology, ix, 9, 14, 43, 53, 61, 68, 81–82, 89, 101
  new, 14, 105
treasury, 4, 7, 11–12, 23, 42
Treasury Department, 48

U

unemployment, x, 11–13, 43, 68
U.S. Treasury, 97–98

W

Wall Street, 95–96
wars, 5, 18, 47, 49, 84
waste, 58, 71
wealth, 11, 13, 19, 22, 25, 27, 31, 33–34, 36–38, 40, 43–44, 51, 96
Wilson, Woodrow, 97

Y

Yellen, Janet, 97

www.ingramcontent.com/pod-product-compliance
Lightning Source LLC
Chambersburg PA
CBHW031922240526
45464CB00022B/644